History of Wisconsin

A Captivating Guide to the History of the Badger State, Starting from the Arrival of Jean Nicolet through the Fox Wars, War of 1812, and Gilded Age to the Present

Free Bonus from Captivating History
(Available for a Limited time)

Hi History Lovers!

Now you have a chance to join our exclusive history list so you can get your first history ebook for free as well as discounts and a potential to get more history books for free! Simply visit the link below to join.

Captivatinghistory.com/ebook

Also, make sure to follow us on Facebook, Twitter and Youtube by searching for Captivating History.

Contents

Introduction

The pristine lakes, towering forests, and breathtaking views of Wisconsin are well-known sights that attract large numbers of tourists every year. Thousands of people flock to Wisconsin each year to hunt in its woods, fish in its waters, or kayak along its many rivers. There are plenty of museums to walk through, too, and much to see within them, from the tragic stories in the Peshtigo Fire Museum to the awe-inspiring sight of the fossilized Boaz mastodon at the University of Wisconsin-Madison.

However, the history of Wisconsin is so much more than just exhibits in museums. The 30th state has a long, rich story behind its modern-day facade. Thousands of years ago, ancient peoples hunted giant beasts on the frozen glaciers that have now given way to rivers and lakes. Rich cultures populated the frigid early forests of Wisconsin, eventually giving way to the arrival of French explorers. Soon, the British took over, ushering in an era of booming colonization, and Wisconsin saw its first recorded war. With the American Revolution, Wisconsin became free, and that brought a whole new set of challenges for its people to face.

This history extends far beyond mere dates and battles. It's a vibrant story filled with fascinating people, like the band of brothers who discovered the bones of a mastodon; the peaceful Jean Nicolet, a

French explorer who became the first European to canoe down Wisconsin's rivers, almost stumbling upon the Mississippi in his quest to find China; Joshua Glover, a slave whose escape made history; Black Hawk, a Sauk chief seeking to protect his people; and Dwight Armstrong, a protester of peace who accidentally took a life. It's filled with fascinating stories, like that of the courageous battle fought by American soldiers against the British near Prairie du Chien during the War of 1812 or the story of the Great Fire of Peshtigo, which would kill more people than any other fire in recorded history.

Wisconsin's history is as richly detailed and relentlessly interesting as its glorious landscapes. Its history has always paralleled that of the United States, giving a fascinating deeper glimpse into a story we all know so well. Wisconsin saw the effects of colonialism, stood up for the rights of all people during the Civil War, and endured the wrath of fire.

And this is its story.

Chapter 1 – Wild Wisconsin

Thousands of years ago, on a windswept tundra, a young man breathed slowly amid the tumbling snowflakes that obscured his vision. The sparse stand of trees was no protection from the icy nip of the wind; he had to resist the urge to reach up and adjust his primitive hood, which was made from animal skin like the rest of his clothing. The fur was thick and warm against his skin, but the wind still found its way inside.

He'd chosen this stand of trees as cover, not from the wind but from the sharp eyes of his prey. Through the film of snowflakes, the enormous beast was still easily visible. A towering creature, it was a great, dark shape on the snowy landscape, its long trunk slightly curled as it moved in long, unhurried strides on its round feet. A dusting of fur rippled in the wind as it moved, and its long tusks were yellow in contrast with the white snow.

The young man took a tighter grip on his atlatl, turning it slightly to glance down at the sharp point of his spear. It was painstakingly made from glittering chalcedony, its edge chipped out to glinting sharpness, both sides fluted for the shaft of the spear to fit perfectly. The mastodon was a mighty creature. It towered over him and weighed several tons. The man thought of his family, of his people. They were a small nomadic group, moving across the untamed world. They were free but easily hungry. This monster would feed them for a long time.

His mind was made up. The young man rushed forth, the atlatl raised. He hurled it with all his strength, an expert movement that sent the shaft of the spear singing through the air. The edge of the chalcedony sliced its way across the distance between the young hunter and the hulking beast. There was a slap, a crunch, and the snow turned scarlet.

The Dosch Brothers and the Boaz Mastodon

More than 10,000 years later, Harry, Chris, Verne, and Clyde strode outside into a world washed clean by rain.

The four brothers were a rowdy gaggle of youthful exuberance. Pushing, shoving, kicking rocks, and cracking jokes, their boisterous voices echoed around a brilliantly green summer landscape. Last night's storm was a distant memory faced with the wonder of this morning. Everything looked brighter than normal: the verdant green of the fields their father owned, which they themselves would someday inherit; the breathtaking blue sweep of the sky; and the rise and fall of the neat fence posts, dug into the ground, planted as firmly as the roots of their family. The boys had grown up on this farm on the banks of Mill Creek. It was in their blood, even though it had only been a little more than 300 years since their ilk first set foot on the continent they now roamed so freely. A continent that had once belonged to an entirely different people.

Right now, though, on June 10th, 1897, the history of humankind in North America was a very long way from the four boys' minds. They were supposed to be checking Mill Creek for flood damage that could threaten the nearby village of Boaz, Wisconsin, but they were far more interested in getting up to any kind of mischief that could bring them some entertainment. Scrambling along the bank, splashing in puddles, and swinging from tree limbs, the boys played their way through the chore that their father had given them.

History doesn't mention which of the boys first spotted the bones. It's clear, though, that just a few minutes later, all four boys were investigating the bank of the creek. The storm had carved out new banks in the night, and it revealed something that instantly piqued the attention of four boys who were looking for something to do on a summer day. As the boys inspected the long white shafts sticking out of the rich earth, they realized these were no ordinary bones. Some of them were thicker than the oldest brother's whole arm.

Such interesting treasures couldn't simply be left in the dirt. Their chore forgotten, the boys set to digging, using rocks and their hands in the soft, wet dirt. It was physical work, but their keen interest and youthful energy prevailed, and soon they'd removed several enormous bones from the mud. They were huge—there was a mighty femur almost as tall as the youngest brother. The boys were fascinated.

Even better was another find: something that looked like an arrowhead. It was a crude thing, chipped out of rock and fluted on both sides. The boys—and, later, many historians—speculated that this must have been what killed the giant beast.

The boys agreed these bones should be exhibited to the general public, as they were objects of curiosity and wonder, far bigger than the bones of any horse or cow. Accordingly, the boys ferried the enormous bones up the banks of the creek all the way to the side of the road. A hitching post had been placed next to the road for the convenience of travelers, and the boys propped the bones up against it. Then they gamboled off, bored and ready for whatever adventure a Wisconsin summer would bring them next. But they didn't leave the "arrowhead" behind. One of the brothers tucked it into his pocket for safekeeping, a special treasure of a splendid boyhood.

It didn't take long for the bones to attract the attention of local newspapers. Journalists from the *Republican Observer*, the *Viola Observer*, and the *Richland Democrat* flocked to photograph the boys and the bones, and they wrote stories about the mysterious origins of these gigantic objects. Recognizing that the bones might be rather more precious than the boys originally thought, their father had them moved to the basement of his great farmhouse.

They didn't remain there for long. An attorney from Wisconsin soon came to the Dosch house and attempted to buy the bones. The boys must have been dismayed, but their father was easily tempted by the exorbitant rate the attorney offered for them: $50, or about $1600 in today's money. For a bunch of apparently worthless bones, it was a huge sum of money for a 19th-century farmer.

The bones were sold to the state of Wisconsin, and in 1915, they were assembled into the skeleton of a long-extinct creature: a mastodon. The skeleton wasn't quite complete, and it took some plaster bones to complete the rest of the body, but it quickly garnered fame for the little village of Boaz. As a result, the beast was named the Boaz mastodon.

The story of the Dosch boys is very much true. The story of the young hunter and his prehistoric prey is an imagining, but, as far as we can tell, it is a fairly accurate one. Fossilization preserved the tale of the human hunter who brought down this massive creature, which would have been closely related to the woolly mammoth and the modern-day elephant, with a chalcedony spearhead.

The Boaz mastodon was displayed in the Geology Museum of the History of Wisconsin in Madison, where it still stands today, although not all of its bones consist of the ones the Dosch boys found in Mill Creek. In fact, the bones of at least two different mastodons contributed to the skeleton. The second mastodon was found at the nearby town of Anderson Mills. Scientists discovered it in 2015, a hundred years after the skeleton was first assembled.

As for the fluted spearhead, it tells far more of that ancient hunter's story than just the bones of his prey. It remained in the possession of the Dosch family until the 1940s when it was mailed to the University of Wisconsin-Madison (two surviving Dosch brothers later identified it as their spearhead in 1966). It is likely responsible for the death of

the mastodon, and it is almost the only evide
earliest human civilization in what is today the st
Clovis culture.

The Clovis people

The Clovis people, so named because then аɪᴜᴀᴄɪɔ .....
discovered in Clovis, New Mexico, is a little-understood culture that
likely inhabited North America in the last few centuries of the Ice
Age. We don't know very much about this mysterious tribe, but
genetic evidence from their fossilized remains suggest they were of
Siberian or Mongolian descent. During the Ice Age, a land bridge
linked modern-day Alaska and Russia over what is today the Bering
Sea, making it possible for humans and animals to cross from Asia
into the Americas. The Clovis most likely came to North America
across the Bering land bridge, where they slowly spread across the
uninhabited continent.

The Wisconsin that the Clovis people inhabited was a very
different landscape from the one that we know today. Instead of a
peaceful woodland inhabited by deer, squirrels, and foxes, Wisconsin,
10,000 years ago, was a fierce, wild tundra where giant mammals
roamed. Alongside the great mastodons, the Clovis also hunted
elephant-like gomphotheres and mammoths, as well as towering
camel-like creatures called camelops. There were also megatherium—
ground sloths bigger than horses—and tapirs. Their distinctive
spearheads, known as Clovis points, were instrumental in their way of
living.

These spearheads are characterized by the grooves chipped on
both sides, which is a process known as fluting. Fluted spearheads
were easier to fit onto shafts, and they also made the shafts more
stable, which made them an efficient weapon when the Clovis worked
together to bring down their enormous prey. It would appear that
fluted spearheads were not something the Clovis brought with them
from their frigid homelands in Siberia, as they have never been found

As well as hunters, the Clovis were innovators, and they came with the idea of the Clovis points themselves.

But their innovations weren't enough to save them. The Clovis numbers declined sharply somewhere around 8,000 BCE, and we're still not sure why. Some theories point to the flooding of Lake Agassiz, a gigantic, prehistoric glacial lake bigger than all of the modern Great Lakes combined. Millions of tons of frigid meltwater flooded into the North Atlantic, triggering a 1,500-year-long cold phase that might have been more than the Clovis could survive.

Another possibility is that the Clovis simply became too numerous, and the population of gigantic mammals that they depended upon so heavily could no longer sustain them. Even thousands of years ago, humanity was already too much for its ecosystem, and the Clovis hunted their prey to extinction, which almost led to their own extinction.

Nonetheless, even though their numbers declined sharply, the Clovis did not entirely disappear. Today, around four-fifths of all modern-day Native Americans are descended from the Clovis.

The Archaic and Woodland Traditions

The Clovis people populated North America in a period that is known as the Paleo-Indian Tradition. It was followed by the Archaic Tradition.

North America's population didn't remain in decline for long. The Clovis were soon followed by other cultures that were very similar to them, such as the Folsom people, who also made fluted spearheads. These were still primitive people, but a great technological leap forward was made when the Old Copper Culture arose. These people had learned the advanced skill of metalwork, extracting the threads of copper from Wisconsin's hills and melting it down to build all kinds of weapons and tools. Their adzes, fishhooks, knives, harpoons, and axes were vastly superior to those of the Paleo-Indians.

However, the Copper Culture, like the Clovis and Folsom, still relied solely on hunting and gathering for their subsistence. They were also largely nomadic, a necessity in the frigid wasteland of Wisconsin at the time. But the world was changing, and around 700 BCE, a new people rose up to make the best of a new world.

When the Old Copper Culture declined in 1000 BCE, Wisconsin was no longer the Arctic tundra of the Paleo-Indians. Instead, it had become one vast and magnificent forest, and the people who lived in it were named after the woods. They are called the Woodland people, and they ushered in the Woodland Period. Unlike the fierce hunters of the Copper Culture, the Woodland people were a deeply settled, peaceful group who put down roots for the first time in North American history.

The Woodland people were influenced by cultures from the south, possibly Mexican people who had come into contact with them in their explorations to the north. This is likely how the Woodland people learned a skill that would change their culture entirely: agriculture. Unlike the nomadic hunter-gatherers of earlier centuries, the Woodland people farmed crops like squash, beans, and corn. They also acquired the skill of pottery-making.

Now that North Americans no longer spent all of their time hunting giant animals in a bid to survive, their beliefs began to grow more complicated, possibly influenced by their South and Central American neighbors. The Woodland people were the first effigy mound builders. By moving millions of cubic feet of earth, they created enormous earthen mounds meticulously shaped like animals or even people. Some of these were used as burial mounds; others may have been spiritual sites for religious rites or ceremonies.

The gentle farmers of the Woodland Period had an extremely peaceful culture. Even though they were one of the first Native American cultures to use the bow and arrow, their weapons were for hunting, not warfare. They had a deeply egalitarian society in which the hierarchy was not central to everyday life. But the gentleness of the Woodland Period could not last forever.

The Mississippian Culture and Aztalan

The Woodland people raised their children, built their mounds, and tilled their fields for nearly 2,000 years until their golden age came to an end toward the late 1ˢᵗ millennium CE.

It all started in what was then a peaceful Woodland village, known today as Aztalan. Built on the banks of the Crawfish River, this little village was a typical Woodland creation. Its people kept cornfields on one side of the village and lived in little conical teepee-like structures built from wooden poles and plaited mats of river grass. They fished, hunted, and lived their ordinary lives in a small, quiet world.

And then the Mississippians came.

The inhabitants of Aztalan were awed by the sight of these strange new visitors. These people were very different from the ever-peaceful Woodland people; they had a strict hierarchy, and the young men who arrived in Aztalan had muscles that were hardened and scarred from warfare instead of agriculture. They shot arrows instead of tilling fields, and their ferocity must have frightened the peaceful Woodland people. However, it would appear that the Mississippians, despite their domineering appearance, were fairly peaceful to their quiet Woodland counterparts. Nonetheless, they'd change Aztalan forever.

These Mississippians were members of a new culture that had originated up and down the banks of the Mississippi River, and they were more advanced than the Woodland people. While they farmed and hunted like the Woodland people, the Mississippians also made war, and their society was more complex. Instead of building sleepy settlements and quiet villages, the Mississippians had built an enormous city in Missouri known as Cahokia. This was an enormous place—a great network of plazas, temples, marketplaces, and effigy mounds—and the Mississippians and Woodland people set out to build Aztalan into something similar.

Over the next few hundred years, Aztalan became a bustling city and a center of trade between the growing populations of the Great Lakes area. While its inhabitants generally lived in wigwams similar to those of the Woodland people, they also built great plazas and wooden platforms for their temples and charnel houses.

Strangely enough, even though the Mississippians were more advanced than the Woodland people, their effigy mounds were far simpler. Instead of constructing intricate mounds in the shapes of deer or birds, they built simple conical burial mounds near Aztalan. Over time, the Mississippians intermarried with the Woodland people until their cultures blended and became one.

Trade boomed in Aztalan, making Wisconsin an important part of Native American society at the time. Goods were brought to Aztalan from other parts of Wisconsin, Missouri, and Illinois. It's likely that Aztalan was also protected by dedicated warriors; in fact, social ranking in Mississippian culture was based solely on prowess in warfare. The strongest soldiers always made their way to the top, which helped the Mississippians survive potential invasions from tribes outside of Wisconsin. However, it also may have proven problematic for ordinary people, as they were essentially governed by bloodthirsty warlords.

The Mississippian Period didn't last long in Wisconsin, or at least not in Aztalan itself. Around 1200 CE, Aztalan was suddenly and mysteriously abandoned. No one knows why. The city was never repopulated by the Native Americans; instead, it was overgrown and returned largely to nature before it was discovered by European settlers in the 19th century. Today, the city lies in Aztalan State Park, a protected area where archaeologists work to understand the ancient cultures of Wisconsin.

The Oneota People

The descendants of the Woodland people lived on even after the abandonment of Aztalan and the decline of the Mississippians. They were called the Oneota people, and they would be the last prehistoric culture to populate North America. They ruled over the Wisconsin wilderness for about 500 years until the arrival of the Europeans.

The Oneota originated as a fairly primitive culture, but as the years passed, they became proficient farmers and builders. Their villages were large and filled with sturdy longhouses and wigwams. Since they built their villages all over Wisconsin, the Oneota engaged in trade and in warfare with each other and with nearby cultures, although they seldom journeyed as far south as Cahokia. They also smoked pipes, which they made from stone, and supplemented their agriculture with fishing and hunting. They were the most populous Native American tribe of Wisconsin during the European Middle Ages.

By the 17th century, Wisconsin had become a very different place than the icy tundra of 8000 BCE. The nomads, who had once hunted giant sloths and mammoths in the snow, were now replaced by farmers, who built longhouses and stone pipes. But the greatest change of all was still to come.

The Europeans were on their way.

Chapter 2 – French Colonization

Illustration I: An early 20th-century depiction of Jean Nicolet

Historians today have little idea of why the Clovis, the Copper Culture, the Woodland people, and the Mississippians declined. Sadly, for the Oneota, it's quite clear why their numbers declined around the 18th century. They suffered the same fate as many other Native Americans in that period: they were pushed out of their homes by the ever-expanding, ever-power-hungry Europeans.

Contrary to popular belief, the first European to set foot in the Americas was not Christopher Columbus. It was a Viking raider, most likely someone under the employ of Leif Eriksson (or Leif Eriksson himself), around 1000 CE. While the Mississippians and Woodland people were building Aztalan, the Vikings were exploring the New World, trading with the natives and fishing in the freezing waters of Greenland, Labrador, and Newfoundland. The Vikings even built a settlement called Vinland in Newfoundland. Its name meant "fertile land," and there was certainly some active trade there. The Vikings sailed along the east coast of North America, and their interactions with the native people seem to have been fairly peaceful. Vinland was abandoned shortly after it was built, and the Vikings never returned. History has lost the reason why.

Nearly 500 years later, the next European would set foot in the Americas. This time, it was Columbus. Columbus was an Italian explorer who was commissioned by the king and queen of Spain to find a trade route to India. His mission was thwarted when it turned out there were two continents in the way. Columbus landed on one of the Caribbean islands in 1492, and although he was convinced that he'd landed in Asia (and remained so for the rest of his life), other explorers followed in his footsteps to convince Europe that they'd found a "New World."

It was the French who became the first Europeans to actively explore inland North America. In 1534, French explorer Jacques Cartier landed in modern-day Canada and launched an expedition into its pristine wilderness. He traveled all the way to modern-day Montreal, and more French soon followed, establishing a fur trading colony known as New France.

In Wisconsin, the Europeans never came into contact with the Oneota themselves, but the steady encroachment of European settlers on Native American territory caused other tribes to flood into the Oneota homeland. The Oneota began to move west, eventually leaving Wisconsin entirely.

Generally, the French attitude toward the Native Americans was more tolerant than the blatant brutality displayed by the Spanish in South America. Samuel de Champlain established the first major fort in Quebec in 1608, decades after Cartier's expedition. He also explored the Nova Scotia and Cape Cod regions.

While the French were certainly hungry for land and power, the prospect of trade with the New World trumped any other early ambitions. They worked to learn Native American languages and established diplomacy with the native tribes, often working and living with the natives in peace. Jean Nicolet is a shining example of a French diplomat who treated the Native Americans as his equals. He set a path that led to decades of peace between most Native American tribes and the French.

Jean Nicolet

Born in 1598, Jean was far from a free-thinking radical. His father was a dispatch carrier in the service of the king of France, a symbol of the so-called *Ancien Régime* that would garner so much hatred during the French Revolution. At the time, France was profoundly Catholic, and its monarchy was profoundly absolute. Serfdom was still a constant reality for its people, and the nation was still deeply entrenched in many of the concepts of the Middle Ages. Religion and monarchy were chief among those concepts, and Jean was deeply loyal to them both.

However, this did not curb his appetite for adventure. Jean was friends with Samuel de Champlain himself, and when Champlain started to look for young men to join him in Canada and expand trade for the French there, Jean jumped at the chance to see the New World. He was only twenty years old when he took the long journey from his hometown in Cherbourg-Octeville all the way to the fort at Quebec in 1618.

The first order of business was for Jean to learn some Native American languages. The Algonquins were some of the most proliferate natives in the area at the time, and they also had very good relations with the French, so Jean was sent to live with a group of them near the Ottawa River. The river was a vital part of the fur trade route, which brought mink, fox, ermine, and other animal skins to France, as the French were constantly hungry for fine fur clothing. This was a lucrative trade, if relentlessly cruel to animals, and the Native Americans actively participated in and likely benefited from it, as they were skilled hunters and trappers themselves who could easily procure pelts and sell them to their new European friends.

While living with the Algonquin, Jean was quick to pick up their language, and he soon discovered that he was very content living among them. In 1620, he was moved to a colony on the shores of Lake Nipissing, which was populated by Algonquin and Odawa. Jean settled effortlessly into life with these peoples. He was content to live there for nearly a decade, and he may have lived there for many more years if it was not for a surprising turn of events.

Jean was a store manager and trader in Lake Nipissing, and he even became a part of the natives' councils, which shows how deeply integrated he was into their society. He was not only a trusted member of their tribe, but he was also a respected leader and an invaluable link between the French settlers of Canada and its native citizens. Jean even fell in love with a Nipissing girl, and the result of their union was a beautiful baby girl named Madeleine Euphrosine Nicolet.

Here, though, it would appear that Jean's old loyalty to the French ways won out over his dedication to his new Nipissing family. After nine years in Lake Nipissing, when Madeleine was still a small child, Jean made the decision that she would be educated as a French child instead of in the traditional Nipissing customs. This may have caused an irreparable rift between Jean and his Nipissing partner. Either way, they split up in 1629, and Jean left Lake Nipissing, never to return.

Jean returned to Quebec with little Madeleine, determined for her to be raised French and given as much of a classical education as a little girl could find in a fur trading colony in the New World. Still, his love of Native Americans did not end, and this was evidenced in the summer of that year. Just as Madeleine was experiencing her first summer among her father's people, tragedy struck Quebec. The Thirty Years' War was raging between most of the European powers at the time, and while this devastating conflict took place mostly within Europe—where it claimed about eight million lives—its far-reaching consequences extended all the way to the New World. The Kirke brothers, a pair of adventurers and traders originally from Scotland, invaded Quebec and conquered it for England, staining a Canadian summer with French blood. The French were forced to flee, and while Champlain went to London, Jean sought refuge with the people he knew best: the Native Americans.

Fleeing with Madeleine to the Lake Huron area, Jean lived among the natives there for three years until Champlain was reinstated as the governor of New France in Quebec. Jean returned to Quebec in 1632, where he lived among the French for a brief time, probably settling Madeleine into a suitable French home, until Champlain called him up with a new mission. Jean was to be sent to establish diplomatic relations with Native Americans again. Only this time, he wouldn't be traveling deeper into Canada. He would be heading south, into the modern-day United States. Into Wisconsin.

Jean Nicolet and the Ho-Chunk

While it had been more than a century since Christopher Columbus set sail to find an alternate trade route to India, many Europeans were still fixated on finding an easy route to China via the Americas. Before the days of the Suez Canal, sailing to Asia was a dangerous and difficult business that could only be achieved by going all the way around the stormy southernmost tip of Africa. Conflict in Eastern Europe made traveling by land equally risky, which made all of Asia's treasures almost priceless in Europe. An easier route to Asia—in particular, India and China—would guarantee almost endless riches to the lucky nation that happened to find that route.

While some exploration of the eastern parts of the Americas taken place, the explorers of the 17th century still had absolu' idea that they were exploring continents instead of mere islands. Legends had been circulating about a mystic route west across North America that would easily take a traveler to the Pacific Ocean and then, by an easy voyage, to China itself.

Champlain was determined to find this fabled "Northwest Passage" for France. Since any explorer lucky enough to find his way through the wild landscape would also have to have excellent diplomatic skills to navigate both the natives and the Chinese, Champlain decided that Jean was the man for the job.

Jean himself had some ideas regarding the Northwest Passage. The Wyandots of Lake Huron had told him about their neighbors to the southwest, the "Puan" people. Since "Puan" translated to "people of the fragrant waters," Jean believed the Puan might be living at the edge of the ocean. That ocean would have to be the Pacific, and if he could reach the Puan, he might just find a route all the way to China.

Champlain was excited about this idea, and he decided to deck Jean out in everything he could need to make it to China. Even though he was a nonviolent man in general, Jean was given a pair of glittering pistols to wear on his belt. A flamboyant Chinese coat, decorated in bright colors and rich embroidery, was placed on his shoulders—an inauspicious garb for a trek through the wilderness, perhaps. Then Jean set off in his canoe across Lake Michigan, looking for China.

Jean canoed all the way into the algae-coated Green Bay, with its distinctive odor rising off its summer waters, becoming the first European to paddle into Wisconsin. His first impression of what would later be called the Badger State was of splendid, untouched woods that towered along the banks of the shimmering bay. Lake Michigan spread out behind him, a mirror in the summer sun. Embroidered coat and all, Jean must have felt very small and very much out of place in his wild and glorious surroundings.

Landing on the shore of smelly Green Bay, it wasn't long before he came across the local Puan. They had never seen a white man before.

How could they? No white man had ever come to Wisconsin before, let alone one decked out in the finery of an embroidered Chinese robe, wielding a pair of flashing pistols. Although it seems unlikely that Jean would have attempted to harm the Puan, perhaps a few shots from the pistols were used to impress them, and he instantly won their respect as he strode through the gun smoke. Jean's diplomacy went far beyond mere flashiness, though, and it wasn't long before he befriended them.

As he picked up on their language, Jean eventually realized his mistake. These people didn't call themselves "Puan." The name he'd translated as meaning "people of the sea" or "people of the fragrant waters" actually meant "people of the stinking waters." It was a derogatory label they'd been given by their enemies farther northeast. It probably referred to the unique aroma of Green Bay, which has, for centuries, been home to blue-green algae blooms that smell none too pleasant.

The people called themselves the Ho-Chunk, or "people of the big voice." It referred to the fact that they considered themselves the progenitors of everyone who spoke their language group, including a nearby tribe called the Menominee, who were equally friendly to explorers.

With that misunderstanding out of the way, Jean was nonetheless determined to find the fabled Northwest Passage and reach the Pacific Ocean. His new friends, the Ho-Chunk, were only too happy to act as his guide to a place where they knew there were wide waters. Accompanied by seven young, strong Ho-Chunk men, Jean set off up the Fox River. He crossed overland a short distance while carrying his canoe and came to the Wisconsin River, which he then followed until he saw a glorious sight. The narrow Wisconsin suddenly widened before him, turning into a great expanse of sparkling water that stretched as far as the eye could see.

Jean was awed, and he was convinced that he'd finally found the Northwest Passage, ensuring rich trade between France and Asia.

Absolutely certain that the water he was looking at belonged to the Pacific, Jean turned back and returned to Green Bay, where he spent the winter with the Ho-Chunk.

Of course, he was nowhere near the ocean. When he'd turned back from the widening water, Jean had still been nearly 2,000 miles away from the Pacific Ocean. The whole of the American West separated him from the sea. What he'd actually discovered was the Upper Mississippi River, the fourth longest river in the world. Just like Columbus, in his search for one treasure, he had been blind to the discovery of another.

Jean ultimately never returned to Green Bay. After returning to Quebec in 1635, he married a Frenchwoman in 1637 and stayed mostly in Canada for the rest of his life. Sadly, this was not a long one. He was only forty-four years old and canoeing happily in the St. Lawrence River, out in the wilderness where his heart had always belonged, when tragedy struck. The canoe capsized, and Jean drowned in the frigid waters of the untamed river.

Pierre-Esprit Radisson and Médard Chouart des Groseilliers

Although Jean Nicolet's news of the discovery of what he thought was the Pacific Ocean was exciting, it was decades before the French could act upon it.

While Nicolet and other diplomats like him had worked hard to maintain good French-Native American relations, the fragile peace crumbled horribly only five years after Jean's return from Wisconsin. The Huron, Algonquin, and other tribes that were loyal to the French were not the only Native Americans to populate the area. The warlike Iroquois were hunters and trappers in Canada and what would become the northern United States. But Europe's insatiable appetite for fur—in particular for beaver pelts—was so enormous that even the great riches of the New World could never hope to satisfy it. Beavers were starting to die out, and the tribes that depended on their pelts for trading to gain access to the Old World's technological wonders—most notably, firearms— began to turn on one another in an attempt to control the dwindling population.

The Iroquois Confederacy was formed when a group of five tribes speaking a similar language came together and decided to root out the French and the other Native American tribes that were allied to them. The Iroquois traded primarily with the Dutch and British, and they started to focus on building up their arsenal, trading pelts for guns instead of tools or food items. And once the Iroquois were on equal footing with the French in terms of weaponry, they struck.

The Beaver Wars lasted for almost sixty years—from the first raids in 1642 to the Great Peace of Montreal in 1701—and devastated the French and their allies, as well as the Iroquois themselves, as the French fought back by burning down crops and villages, causing many Iroquois to starve. The greatest atrocities were suffered by the French-allied Native Americans. Entire tribes were decimated by the war, some of them to the point of extinction.

For twenty years, Wisconsin was left alone by the Europeans, but it was not immune to the changes caused by the Beaver Wars. Since there were no colonial settlements in the area, it was a comparatively safe place for the peaceful tribes who were being driven from their homes by the brutal Beaver Wars. Wisconsin became a haven for displaced tribes to live away from the conflict.

Seven years after the death of Jean Nicolet, the next French explorer to delve into the wilderness of Wisconsin came to the New World: Pierre-Esprit Radisson.

Pierre was most likely born in 1636, which means he was only fifteen or sixteen when he journeyed from his birthplace near Avignon to explore New France. He was likely accompanied by his half-sister, Marguerite. They settled in the town of Trois-Rivières on the banks of the very same river that had claimed Jean Nicolet's life. The region was a wonderland of thrills and beauty, perfect for an adventurous teenager. Pierre hunted, fished, swam, and explored with his peers. It was on one of these happy wanderings that Pierre blundered right into the lap of France's great enemy: members of the Iroquois Confederacy. The Mohawk tribe had just attacked and killed a number of Frenchmen when Pierre stumbled upon them, and they fell upon the boy. However, instead of killing him, the Mohawks decided to take him home to their people.

Because Pierre was young, he was kidnapped instead of being executed, and a Mohawk family adopted him as their own child, which was a long-standing tradition of the tribe. As the weeks passed, Pierre became quite comfortable in his new family. He picked up the Mohawk language and customs, and he was treated like any other young Mohawk boy, joining hunting parties and exploring the wilderness of what was probably modern-day New York State.

While out hunting, Pierre had his first contact with a non-Mohawk person since his kidnapping. He came upon an Algonquin, who immediately recognized him as being a Frenchman. Appalled to see a French boy living among the Iroquois, the Algonquin man fell upon the Mohawks and killed them, convincing Pierre to come home to his own people in Trois-Rivières. Pierre agreed, and they traveled together for a time until the Iroquois came upon them and recognized Pierre as an adopted Mohawk. Incensed by his treachery, they killed the Algonquin man and brought Pierre back to the Mohawks, where he was punished by torture.

Pierre would have likely died slowly and in terrible pain if it wasn't for the Mohawk family who had been caring for him. His adoptive family acted as advocates for him, snatching him from the very jaws of death and even offering financial compensation to the families of the people whom Pierre's Algonquin ally had killed. Pierre was returned to his adoptive family, and he was given a new name: Ovinha.

Pierre was so deeply touched by this gesture that he remained with the Mohawks by choice for several months afterward, even declining an offer from a fellow Frenchman who wanted to pay a ransom in order to "save" him from the Mohawks.

Eventually, though, the memories of Pierre's torture, which included having a hot nail driven through his foot and having his fingernails pulled out, came to haunt him. He slipped out of the Mohawk village early one morning, probably around 1653, and returned to the French.

By the time Pierre met Marguerite's new husband, Médard Chouart des Groseilliers, he was already a seasoned adventurer. In about 1659, the two men decided that an expedition across Lake Michigan and into Green Bay was well overdue. Like Jean, they took canoes across Lake Michigan, and this time, they journeyed as far as Lake Superior. There was an abundance of natural resources here, as well as people who were relatively untouched by the Beaver Wars that were still raging elsewhere in New France. Above all else, there were more than enough beaver pelts to be had. Pierre and Médard realized that they were going to be incredibly rich.

The two men returned in 1660, accompanied by natives in around 300 canoes, carrying a wealth of beaver pelts. The French governor was incensed. Thanks to the fact that Pierre and Médard hadn't been given permission to take their journey, he fined them heavily and seized all of their pelts, which must have given him a healthy little profit.

Pierre and Médard eventually switched sides. They worked for the British and eventually established the lucrative Hudson Bay Company in modern-day Canada. They had established that Wisconsin was rich in natural resources and peaceful people. The Ho-Chunk and Menominee, who had welcomed Jean Nicolet so openly, were just as friendly with Pierre and Médard. Even the Santee Dakota, who had never been in contact with Europeans before, proved to be friendly.

Claude Jean Allouez, Jacques Marquette, and Louis Jolliet

The next Frenchman to journey into Wisconsin arrived five years later, and while the previous Frenchmen to reach this wilderness had been seeking monetary gain, Claude Jean Allouez had very different motives.

Claude had been ordained as a Jesuit priest in 1655 after spending his youth studying in Toulouse. He'd come to New France not to seek his fortune but to preach his religion, and the untouched wilderness of Wisconsin seemed like a fertile field in which to sow his message. Claude was the first European to build a permanent settlement in the Wisconsin area. He established a peaceful relationship with the Potawatomi, evangelizing many members of the tribe and building a mission in the Green Bay area. Claude would build numerous mission stations throughout the area, such as the St. Francis Xavier Mission near modern Oconto and another at De Pere.

While Claude was not the explorer that Nicolet, Radisson, and des Groseilliers had been, he played an important role in establishing peaceful relations with the Native Americans, especially the Potawatomi. He also kept a detailed journal of the landscape and of his activities, gathering useful knowledge that was indispensable to two famous explorers who would later follow in his footsteps.

Claude was rapidly bringing Jesuit missionaries to Wisconsin, establishing many of them at De Pere as some of Wisconsin's first semi-permanent settlers, when two explorers arrived, determined to finish the journey that Jean Nicolet had begun in 1634. It was now 1673, nearly forty years later, and no one had gone as far down the Wisconsin River as Nicolet had. These two men were Louis Jolliet and Jacques Marquette, and they were ready for adventure and, they hoped, to finish the journey all the way to China itself.

Of course, even though Jolliet and Marquette traveled in Nicolet's footsteps all the way from the Fox River to the Wisconsin River, they never reached the Pacific. They reached the Mississippi instead and discovered that it was an enormous river, one that would be vitally important in the history of the country they were exploring—a country that would eventually become known as the United States of America.

The whitewater rapids that Jolliet and Marquette encountered where the Wisconsin met the Mississippi would later be known as Prairie du Chien, and it became the site of the very first fort to be occupied by Europeans year-round in Wisconsin. It was built by a fellow Jesuit: Nicolas Perrot.

Nicolas Perrot

Like Pierre-Esprit Radisson, Nicolas Perrot was just sixteen years old when he took the long journey from France to New France in 1660. At nineteen, he'd already established himself as a fur trader, speaking the native languages skillfully, but trade was not his only ambition. Nicolas wanted to reach the very edge of the frontier, and he wanted to be a diplomat too.

In 1668, when he'd gained some experience as a fur trader, Nicolas came to Wisconsin for the first time. The Jesuit missionaries had established themselves in the area by that point, but many of them only stayed in Wisconsin for a few months at a time; they did not live in the area permanently. Nicolas's first goal was to trade with the peaceful Potawatomi, but he reached Wisconsin to find them in conflict with another Native American tribe, the Menominee. Both tribes had been in regular contact with the Europeans, and when Nicolas arrived, he was a neutral party who could communicate with them both. With a bit of skillful diplomacy, Nicolas was able to settle the dispute between the tribes, winning the respect of both the French and Native Americans.

Nicolas didn't stay in Wisconsin for long. He returned to New France in 1670, and it would be fifteen years before he saw the shores of Lake Michigan again. This time, it would be to come there to stay. Remembering his solid relations with the natives of the area, the French governor sent Nicolas to Wisconsin to establish year-round settlements for French traders. The first of these was Fort St. Nicolas, which he built in 1685 beside the rushing rapids of Prairie du Chien. Fort St. Antoine and Fort Perrot were built near Lake Pepin.

For the next three or four decades, Wisconsin enjoyed peace, as its European citizens set about trading and engaging in missionary work, not violence. It was during this time that the first Africans came to

Wisconsin. They were slaves who had been imported by their French masters.

Although the buildings Perrot established were referred to as "forts," there was nothing military about these primitive and remote outposts. They were merely storerooms and meeting points for fur traders to conduct their business year-round. While they did serve to stave off the ever-encroaching Iroquois, they did not hold garrisons of soldiers. Still, Wisconsin mostly experienced peace apart from the odd Iroquois raid.

Sadly, this peace couldn't last forever. Enemies were coming, and this time, their attacks would come from both Europeans and Native Americans.

Chapter 3 – British Colonization

To the Meskwaki tribe at Little Lake Butte des Morts, the sight of a little flotilla of white men in canoes was not a strange one. The year was 1730; it had been more than a century since the fur trade had begun between the Native Americans of the Wisconsin region and the French who colonized it. The Meskwaki guards were heavily armed, but their minds were filled with opportunity as they watched the canoes paddling down the Fox River toward them.

The Meskwaki themselves never traded directly with the French. They used their allies, a neutral tribe called the Sauk, for that. They sold their furs to the Sauk, who then sold them to the French. The Meskwaki had seldom ever trusted anyone, even among the other Native American tribes. So, trading with the French was out of the question.

That didn't mean they couldn't get anything out of the French, though. The Meskwaki had been controlling the banks of the Fox River for so long that they were also known as the Fox Indians; the river and the people were practically inseparable. And since the Fox was an important waterway for the fur trade, as it was a vital means of traveling long before Wisconsin was crisscrossed with roads, the Meskwaki saw the French traders as an easy way of asserting their dominance and lining their pockets.

As the French canoes came closer to the bank, the guards were ready to receive the tribute that all traders owed them when they crossed through Meskwaki lands. The canoes were promisingly full; they could see the cargo bulging beneath their oilskin coverings. The waterproof oilskin would protect whatever was inside, and the Meskwaki were eager to get their share. The French had brought all kinds of wonders to Wisconsin, such as steel, flint, and firearms. These were objects that many Native Americans could no longer function without.

The canoes drew nearer, and the Meskwaki leaned forward in anticipation of rich French gifts. That was when everything went horribly wrong. The oilskins were thrown back, and the peaceful air was shattered by the crashing rhythm of gunfire. Grapeshot peppered the air, pounding into the ranks of the unwitting Meskwaki. Blood soaked into the riverbank, spraying onto the guards from their fallen comrades as a swivel gun on one of the canoes spat death onto the riverbank.

One by one, the oilskins were cast back from the canoes, and soldiers scrambled to their feet from where they'd been hiding in the shallow bellies of the craft. Raising muskets to their shoulders, they fired into the Meskwaki, sending plumes of white gun smoke into the air. Some of the tribesmen stood and fought as the French advanced; some fled, but even they could find no sanctuary. As they ran into the woods, more Frenchmen appeared from behind their lines. There was nowhere to run. The air seemed thick with bullets, the ground slick with blood. They were stumbling over their fallen kindred as they sought survival.

The entire Meskwaki tribe was put to flight. They abandoned their village, the children screaming in their parents' arms as the tribe disappeared into the woods. Well, what was left of the tribe. And it wasn't much.

The Fox Wars

The bloody battle at Little Butte des Morts in 1730 was only one of many vicious conflicts that took place during the Second Fox War, which was fought between the French and the Meskwaki tribe for twenty-four years.

This was a conflict that had been brewing for a long time, and it was accordingly strong and bitter. Things between the Meskwaki and the French had never been peaceful. "Meskwaki" was their own name for their tribe; it meant "red earth," as their belief was that they had been created from the rich, red soil that lined the river where they made their home. The French mistranslated the word, calling them the "Fox Tribe" instead.

The Meskwaki had been battling with many of their neighboring tribes for centuries. Among these were the Chippewa, who were very friendly with the French. This immediately made the French suspicious of the Meskwaki. To make matters worse, as the French probed deeper and deeper into Meskwaki territory, the Meskwaki started to draw nearer to the Iroquois, trading with them and the British instead of the Sauk and French. Tension grew between the tribes, and matters were only made worse when the Meskwaki started exacting tribute on the French traders passing through their territory.

Things came to a head in 1712 after decades of rising tension. Detroit, Michigan, was only a settlement then, but it was an important foothold for the French, a tiny oasis of civilization in what they viewed as a landscape peopled only by barbarians. The Meskwaki launched an open attack on the settlement. The outnumbered French were in dire straits, and it would have been an easy Meskwaki victory if it wasn't for the fact that the French had cultivated excellent relationships with other native tribes. Native allies of the French rushed to the rescue, and the Meskwaki were all but decimated.

The Meskwaki tribe had not been a large one to start with. By this point, there were only around 1,500 Meskwaki, and they knew they couldn't openly attack the French again. However, since they stuck to their policy of demanding tribute from traders passing down the Fox River, the Meskwaki still garnered plenty of unwanted attention from the French. Numerous small knots of French soldiers were sent to attack the Meskwaki, each time resulting in a short-lived and uneasy peace. The treaty would always end up being broken, and the Meskwaki and the French would find themselves in conflict once again.

It was in 1730 that the war became truly serious with the surprise attack at Little Butte des Morts, located near modern-day Menasha. The leader of the attack, Captain Pierre Paul Marin de la Malgue, was an established military leader with little regard for anything but victory. His attack was not simply a military defeat for the Meskwaki; it was practically genocide. Their tribe, which had already been dwindling by this point, shrunk horribly in a single bloody night. Those who did survive the attack could no longer stay in their ancestral home; they fled, leaving their dead to rot in the sun, and traveled to the Wisconsin River. Once they realized they were not being followed, they paused to rest at Wauzeka. One account tells of the discovery of a cave filled with human bones at this location a few decades later. It is speculated that these bones are the remains of the wounded Meskwaki who'd made it to Wauzeka after the attack but could go no farther.

At any rate, the Meskwaki couldn't return to their homes on the Fox River. They sheltered at Wauzeka for the winter instead, hoping they'd be left alone now that they were no longer badgering the French traders for tribute. Their hopes were sorely misplaced. Marin, their nemesis, was still watching them. In the depths of winter, he waited for the Meskwaki men to head out of their new village on a hunting expedition and then attacked. Capturing the women, children, and elderly, he refused to release them back to their people unless the men promised that the Meskwaki would leave Wisconsin forever.

Driven out by the French, the Meskwaki wandered out of the home that had been theirs for generations. According to some sources, this was not the first time the Meskwaki found themselves displaced; they may have been driven into Wisconsin by the Chippewa generations before, a possibility that would have led to their poor relations with the latter tribe. At any rate, this time, their displacement almost led to their total extinction. By 1733, there were only around 500 Meskwaki left alive. They had no choice but to join forces with the only friends they had left: the Sauk. Although the Sauk lived around Green Bay, the French finally left the Meskwaki alone now that they had joined with a friendly tribe.

The Sauk, too, would find themselves displaced not too far in the future. As Europeans continued to flood into Wisconsin, space and resources became tighter and tighter. Green Bay was getting crowded, and the Sauk left it behind, moving nearer to Prairie du Chien around 1780. They would only settle there for around half a century. Eventually, like many other native tribes of the eastern United States, they would have to cross the Mississippi into a foreign new world, driven by the tide of Europeans flowing into the lands they had lived in for thousands of years.

However, by that time, the Europeans filling Wisconsin were no longer Frenchmen. French control of Wisconsin was coming to an end—and it would be a brutal and bloody one.

The French and Indian War

As the 18th century slipped into its second half, the New World was suddenly beginning to feel smaller than before. British colonies had been established on the eastern coast for more than a century, and their ever-growing towns were starting to burst at the seams. Older colonies, such as Virginia and Plymouth, had been expanding at an exponential rate when their growth had to come to a grinding halt.

The majority of North America still stretched out to the western horizon, tantalizing and unexplored, its enormity almost incomprehensible to the pioneers living at the borders of their colonies. But to the British colonists, there was no way to get to it. To the north, they were hemmed in by the French; to the south, by the

Spanish; to the east, by the ocean. And although no one had explored the West, the French controlled a long section of waterways that connected their territories in modern-day Canada to their southernmost colony in Louisiana.

The French and British had been in almost constant conflict for the entirety of the 18th century. In a brooding, bloody manner reminiscent of the Hundred Years' War during the late Middle Ages, the French and British had been squabbling almost constantly, sometimes in outright warfare and sometimes in proxy wars. In these proxy wars, other countries would come into the conflict, and each of the great warring nations would choose a side to ally themselves with, just for an excuse to fight one another. Europe was war-torn as a result, and many of these wars had effects on the colonies.

But in the 1750s, for the very first time, a war fought in the colonies would spill over into the ancestral motherlands.

It started around 1754/55 when the French began to push farther and farther into the Ohio River Valley, which was then colonized by the British. Small spats started up between the colonists. These eventually caught the attention of the military, and by 1756, open war had broken out—a war that would see a young officer named George Washington commanding troops.

The French colonies were wildly outnumbered by the British. Of the French, there were only around 60,000; the British numbered over a million. But the French had one great advantage. Instead of alienating themselves from the natives surrounding them, they had, for the most part, forged powerful alliances with them. The Meskwaki were an exception. Most of the native tribes that came in contact with the French were happy to trade with them and, now, to go to war with them. Backed by numerous Native American tribes, the outnumbered French not only held their own against the British, but they also defeated them in the early battles. George Washington was forced to drink deeply of the bitter draft of defeat in what would become known as the French and Indian War.

However, in 1757, everything changed. William Pitt was made the commander of the British royal forces in the New World, and unlike the previous commander, he saw the conflict with the French as being vitally important. The Seven Years' War had broken out in Europe, which was intimately connected with the French and Indian War. If the British could secure a victory in the New World, Pitt believed that winning in Europe would be that much easier. Despite the fact that he didn't actually go to the New World, his command proved excellent. He threw all the resources he had into the war, putting his country deeply into debt to do so, and quickly began to see results.

The first great British victory was fought in 1758 when the French were routed in the Battle of Louisburg. Only a year later, the Battle of Quebec saw the French completely driven out of one of their oldest colonies in Canada. This was a hard-fought battle that cost both sides their commanders. The French were left clinging to their last foothold in Canada: Montreal. Even that did not remain for long.

Back in the Old World, the conflict was no less brutal. The War of the Austrian Succession earlier in the century had left many loose ends untied, and the French and British were fighting each other heavily, dragging so many other nations into the fight that it has since been regarded as one of the earliest world wars.

The Hundred Years' War had not been dissimilar. There, too, the French had shined in early victories, but as it wore on, the British rose, eventually bringing France to its knees. Yet, in the end, a French peasant maiden named Joan of Arc, unarmed and on a white horse, bearing a white banner, led all of France to victory and thrust the British out of the country completely.

This time, though, there was no Joan of Arc. There would be no Hail Mary for the French. In 1760, Montreal fell, leaving Canada almost completely in British hands. One year later, the war reached even as far as the comparatively unimportant settlements of Wisconsin. The British attacked Green Bay, and although the French and their allies—among them, the Ho-Chunk, Sauk, and Chippewa—

fought bravely to defend it, they stood no chance against the imperial British Army. Green Bay fell in 1761, leaving Wisconsin in British hands.

Wisconsin itself was seldom used as a battleground for the French and Indian War. Nonetheless, the war would change the fate of this territory forever. When the Treaty of Paris was signed in 1763, bringing an end to the French and Indian War in the colonies and the Seven Years' War in Europe, it would change the fates of many colonies all the way from Cuba to Canada. While the French were allowed to hold on to Louisiana (and would continue to do so until the time of Napoleon, decades later), Canada, Florida, and Wisconsin were all ceded to the British.

Wisconsin was now a British colony. Its peaceful era of the French fur trade was over. A time of far more aggressive European settlement had begun.

Wisconsin under the British

While it had been more than a hundred years since Claude Jean Allouez built the first settlements in Wisconsin that would be peopled by Europeans year-round, there were still no real permanent European settlers in the area. The majority of the Europeans who came to Wisconsin were still either fur traders or missionaries, and they stayed for a year here or there but were usually quick to return to the more established colonies of the New World or even to Europe itself.

It was only when Wisconsin became a British colony that the first lifelong settlers started to come to the area. While we can't be sure who the first permanent settler in Wisconsin was, the honor is usually attributed to Charles Michel de Langlade. He was a lieutenant for the French in the French and Indian War, and he was perhaps uniquely equipped to unite the French and their native counterparts. His father was French, but his mother was an Ottawa, and Charles had grown up fighting the Chickasaw alongside his Ottawa uncle. He had none of the fear of Native Americans that many British harbored, and he was happy to move to Green Bay in 1764, where he set up a trading post. He would later serve as an officer in the American Revolutionary War.

The British, however, were interested in their new territory, and they wanted to know much more about it. While heroes like Jean Nicolet had explored vast tracts of Wisconsin's wilderness, large parts of the area had never been mapped. All that changed in 1766 with the arrival of Jonathan Carver, an adventurer to the marrow of his bones.

Born in Massachusetts, Jonathan was a born and bred British American, combining a thirst for the unknown with a loyalty to the British Crown. By the time he was sent on his Wisconsin expedition, Jonathan was a captain in the military and a father of seven children. He'd been approached by Robert Rogers and Captain James Tute, who persuaded him that the British Crown had authorized an expedition into the Great Lakes area and that the government would pay him handsomely for his efforts. Jonathan was only too happy to venture into the wilderness for money.

Jonathan spent several years adventuring throughout the Great Lakes area, following the Minnesota River deeper into Wisconsin than most white men had ever dared to go. He was searching, like Nicolet, for the Northwest Passage; instead, he found a wealth of pristine wilderness and a vast array of fascinating indigenous peoples. Spending months among the Dakota (who would later be displaced to the Great Plains when Europeans continued to flood into their Wisconsin home), Jonathan kept a detailed journal, drawing intricate maps of Wisconsin that were so outstanding that many considered them to be a work of fiction only to find out later that they were the solemn truth.

This confusion was in part due to the fact that Rogers and Tute had never actually obtained authorization from the Crown to launch their expedition. When Jonathan Carver returned to Fort Michilimackinac to meet with Rogers, it wasn't long before British soldiers arrived to arrest Rogers. He was later charged with treason, and while John was never arrested, he was also denied any form of payment. He'd spent years in the wilderness to not even see a bent penny for his efforts. In fact, it took him years to raise funds to publish his journals, a mission that became the main focus of his life and took him all the way back to London, leaving his wife and children in the New World. He would never see his family again, as he would die in England in 1780.

While Jonathan Carver's story is tragic, many other settlers found success, fortune, and happiness in Wisconsin. British colonists flooded into Green Bay and Prairie du Chien, establishing ever-growing colonies that eventually became villages, then towns. By 1780, Green Bay had become an active community. Children ran in the streets and roamed in the woods. Green Bay was no longer a rough frontier town composed of adventurous young men and courageous missionaries. It was now a village of families, a place where entire lives could be lived from screaming infanthood to quiet old age. The fur trade, of course, was booming, but the earth also felt the bite of British plows for the first time. Farms were established, alongside other businesses like stores, blacksmiths, and all the other services that were needed to keep a town prosperous.

And Green Bay not only prospered—it flourished. Now almost entirely self-sufficient, its people were no longer constantly occupied with spartan survival. They were even beginning to hold dances and festivities on special occasions.

Europeans were not the only people coming to Wisconsin either. Africans had been pouring into the New World as slaves for centuries, but as the 18th century drew toward its close, freedmen were becoming more common. In 1791, two such African Americans established a trading post in modern-day Marinette near Green Bay. They lived peacefully among the Menominee tribe, trading in furs a long way from where they had been captured and oppressed.

Green Bay wouldn't remain a British colony for long. In fact, it belonged to the British for exactly twenty years, after which another

Treaty of Paris would transfer it once again. And this time, none of the old colonial powers would control it.

Wisconsin was about to become part of a free America.

Chapter 4 – Wisconsin as a United States Territory

Illustration II: A monument to the Battle of Stillman's Run, the first of the Black Hawk War

By July 19th, 1814, Lieutenant Joseph Perkins knew that Fort Shelby was doomed.

It seemed such a pitiful thing: a little wooden construction only big enough for its garrison of sixty Americans, perched on the edge of the colony that was growing at Prairie du Chien. There were no trappers walking the hills or tradesmen prowling the street this summer, though. The war had taken so much, and for the first time, it was about to take a piece of Wisconsin too.

Lieutenant Perkins had been aware from the start that the odds weighed heavily against the Americans. The British who had besieged them in Fort Shelby outnumbered his men nearly ten to one, between themselves and their Native American allies. It had been two days since the British had first attacked. They'd first come up the Mississippi with their three gunboats on July 17th, and that was when Lieutenant Perkins still had a gunboat of his own. Even though it had only fourteen oars, the *Governor Clark* was a sturdy little vessel, and Perkins had hoped that it could hold its own against the British.

It did, but only for about two hours. Knowing immediately that the gunboat was the Americans' only hope, the British turned their fire on the *Governor Clark*. Shells punched into its wooden flanks, ripping ugly holes into its innards, sending the muddying river water flooding into its guts. Reduced to a hulking wreck of wood splinters, the *Governor Clark* had no choice but to drift downriver, away from the relentless onslaught of the British.

That left Perkins and his men stranded and alone in their tiny fort. Somehow, despite the constant pounding of the shells that shook the walls of Fort Shelby and made the ground tremble as the men moved around within, they held out for a full two days. Lieutenant Colonel William McKay, the British commander, was almost leisurely in his steady pounding of the fort; he knew it had to fall sooner or later. It was a pitiful thing, defended by a mere handful of people, compared to the might of his gunboats.

Perkins' men fought courageously, but Perkins knew that the loss of Prairie du Chien would leave Wisconsin almost undefended against the approaching British. It was scarcely colonized, yet its resources were valuable, and he knew that the Americans needed everything they could get to win this war—or even to survive it. But by July 19ᵗʰ, the situation had gotten desperate.

Fort Shelby's well had quite literally run dry.

The well was situated within the fort itself, and for two days, it had been supplying the men with clean, fresh water, but its supply was by no means limitless. Parched fighting men in the hot summer had depleted it to its very dregs. Perkins had sent men into the well to dig deeper, but that had only made matters worse. The entire well collapsed, replacing their source of life-giving fluid with a crumbling heap of rock and earth.

Perkins was desperate, and Fort Shelby was doomed. And to make matters worse, McKay was growing impatient. Tired of wasting ammunition on this puny fort, he started to fire cannonballs that were so hot they glowed scarlet. Wherever they tore into Fort Shelby, they set the tinder-dry wood alight. In minutes, the fort was wrapped in flames.

And as much as Lieutenant Joseph Perkins wanted to save his country, he also had to save his men. So, he did the only thing he could have done.

He surrendered.

The American Revolutionary War

Joseph Perkins and his men fought a bitter battle that would have been almost incomprehensible right after the French and Indian War. In the mid- to late 18ᵗʰ century, Americans *were* British. The men and women who colonized America fought shoulder-to-shoulder with British-born soldiers in the French and Indian War. Great Britain was the motherland going to war for its colonies; it saw itself as the savior of its people who lived abroad. And while the Americans had escaped doom thanks to Great Britain's assistance, they would soon have reason to be discontent with their status as a British colony.

The Battle of Prairie du Chien, which was fought in the dry summer of 1814, was part of the second war that the Americans and British would fight against each other. The first was one of the most incredible turning points of history: the American Revolutionary War of 1775-1783.

The French and Indian War had secured the borders of America against the French, added Canada to the British Empire, and made Florida and Wisconsin American territories. For many colonists, life had improved. However, the aftermath was devastating, and it was all thanks to the British Crown's treatment of its colonists.

William Pitt had only been able to win the war against the French and Native Americans because of his heavy investment in the struggle. By then, Great Britain had already been all but penniless, stripped of its wealth by the Seven Years' War in Europe. Pitt had had no choice but to borrow tremendous sums of money, and when the French and Indian War was over, Great Britain found itself massively in debt. The British reasoned that the debt had been incurred to protect the citizens of the Thirteen Colonies, conveniently forgetting that a large part of the British economy depended on activities in North America. They believed that paying off the debt should be a burden laid almost solely on the shoulders of the colonists.

Since there was no colonial representation in the British Parliament, numerous acts were passed that bore tremendously heavy taxes upon the colonists, who had themselves suffered hugely during the war. Among others, the Stamp Act and the Tea Act made many simple items of daily use almost unaffordable to the ordinary American. The economy struggled, and so did everyday people, as they had to labor to pay these exorbitant taxes. The fact that the colonists had no one in their corner in Parliament bred bitter resentment. They had no legal recourse against the perceived injustices laid upon them, and discontent was rife in the colonies.

Protests started to break out in the cities, as citizens began to demand that their voices be heard in the only way they could. It was in 1770, five years before the war was actually declared, that the first blow of the American Revolution was struck. A mob of colonists moving along King Street in Boston was growing increasingly restless as they chanted, "No taxation without representation!" They approached the Custom House on King Street, which was guarded by a single British soldier. The protest started to turn into a fight, and when other soldiers arrived and fired heavily into the largely unarmed crowd, the fight turned into a tragedy. Five ordinary colonists were killed, and six others were wounded. The event became known as the Boston Massacre.

Boston was once again the setting for another event that would trigger the revolution. Three years later, discontent was still rising, particularly over the exorbitant taxes placed on tea. On December 16th, 1773, a British East India Company ship was lying at anchor in Griffith's Wharf, Boston. It was loaded down with 342 chests of tea, worth about $1 million. Sick of the Tea Act, some colonists stormed the ship dressed as Mohawk warriors, seized the chests, and dumped them all into the sea. The Boston Tea Party was by no means as bloodthirsty as the massacre that preceded it, but it was a powerful sign that no amount of gunfire would quell the colonists' thirst for justice.

However, instead of listening to reason, the British Crown reacted by clamping down heavily on the Americans, as if they were determined to tax them into submission. A series of acts followed that would become known as the Coercive Acts. Boston's port was closed, bringing an abrupt halt to the trade with Britain, which had been America's lifeblood since its earliest colonization; the citizens of Great Britain were made immune to criminal prosecution, allowing them to do as they pleased with their American counterparts; and colonists were forced to provide lodging in their own personal homes for British soldiers.

While negotiations were attempted, a peaceful outcome was never reached. The British wouldn't budge. The time was ripe for a rebellion, and numerous rebel organizations began to pop up, talking for the first time of independence from the motherland. Secret caches of weapons were made. War was on the horizon.

In response, Great Britain poured more soldiers into North America, determined to subdue it by any means necessary. If taxation hadn't worked, perhaps bullets would. One such troop of British soldiers caught wind of a stockpile of weapons in Concord in April 1775. Mobilizing quickly, a huge regiment of British troops headed for the town of Concord, Massachusetts, on April 18th.

A group of American rebels were made aware of the British march and knew that they had to send word to Concord to avoid the stockpile being seized. Horsemen in the moonlight raced across the state to issue their warning, Paul Revere among them. Only one, Samuel Prescott, managed to reach Concord, doing so in the early hours. The militiamen managed to secure their weapons and were parading as a show of force when the British arrived.

It would appear that there was no intention of actually starting a battle on that day, but a battle did begin. To this day, it's unclear whether it was a British or an American soldier who fired the first shot of the American Revolution, but that shot rang out nonetheless, with an echo that would ring through history forever. The fight began, and open war had begun. It would last for eight long and bloody years.

With George Washington as commander-in-chief, the Americans quickly gained an advantage, expelling the British from Boston in 1776. While sheltering in Canada, the British planned to hit New York first. For the Americans, the fight had long since stopped being about taxation or representation. They would never again be content to be crushed under the heel of British oppression or count themselves a part of the British Empire. America wanted to be free. Accordingly, the Declaration of Independence was signed on July 4th, 1776.

In a matter of weeks, the British launched their invasion. Huge numbers of British troops arrived in New York and began to systematically work their way through the colonies, their sheer numbers and vast resources constantly beating back the Americans. For the Americans, 1777 was a year of one defeat after another. Despite the fact that the French were quietly slipping aid to the Americans in secret, the British seemed indomitable. The war might have ended there, and the United States of America might never have existed if it wasn't for the two Battles of Saratoga in September and October 1777. These ended with the surrender of an entire British force, marking a powerful American victory.

The French openly entered the war in 1778, once again using a proxy war to strike against the British, something they had been doing almost uninterrupted since the Middle Ages. Although French training and resources were an invaluable help to the colonists, the year 1778 did not bring the victory that the Americans hoped for. The year ended with a stalemate in the North; in the South, one disaster led to another, leading to two years of repeated defeats for the Americans there.

Exhausted of bloodshed, by 1780, many of the American troops had seen five years of a war that was beginning to look utterly hopeless. Mutiny and desertion began to spark up among the American troops, most famously when General Benedict Arnold defected to the British. He had been a hero early in the war, but he would go down in history as a heinous traitor. Piece by piece, town by town, the British were gaining ground in the South, pushing the Americans back.

Things began to change at last in 1781. French training and support were starting to pay off, and what was more, General Nathanael Greene was given command of the American armies in the South. Although Greene was never known for any glittering victories, his maneuvers through the Carolinas forced the British toward the coastline, which would be their ultimate downfall.

As the year wore on and as the weary troops clashed time and time again, the war began to draw to a close. Greene and French General Marquis de Lafayette had spread the British commander, General Charles Lord Cornwallis, and his forces against the sea on Virginia's coast. General George Washington himself commanded a great fleet from Connecticut, arriving on Cornwallis's shoreline on September 19th, 1781. The Battle of Yorktown was a short-lived one, and it inevitably ended in Cornwallis's surrender.

With that, the Americans effectively won their independence, although the war would officially continue for another two years. There were no more major battles and few hostilities, although British troops stayed in New York and Charleston until a treaty was signed. This was the second Treaty of Paris, which was signed in 1783.

Those last two years had been filled with negotiations, and Britain, thoroughly thrashed by its own colonies, had found itself in a deeply humbling position. Not only would the Americans be paying no more taxes to the Brits, but they would also no longer be a part of the British Empire either. Britain had to recognize the Declaration of Independence and signed away any of its rights to America. The United States of America was born in blood.

In Wisconsin itself, there was little fighting, but the implications of the war were enormous. In as much time as it takes for a child to become a man, Wisconsin had gone from being a French colony to a British colony. Now, it was considered the possession of America, although it would only become an official territory in 1836.

The American Revolutionary War had not shed much blood in Wisconsin itself, but the war that followed—America's "second war of independence"—was a very different story.

The War of 1812

After the American Revolutionary War, the newly independent United States began to find its feet as a nation in its own right. Despite covering a vast area of territory, the US was still heavily reliant on trade with the Old World, especially with its revolutionary ally of France.

Unfortunately for the US, Great Britain and France had still not let go of their centuries-old conflict. The Hundred Years' War and the Seven Years' War had left tensions boiling, and as the 19th century arrived, Great Britain found itself plunged into some of its bloodiest battles with France. These were the Napoleonic Wars. In a bid to cripple the French, Great Britain's powerful navy began to overrun most of the world's seas, restricting trade with France as much as possible.

For the US, this meant that trade with France was growing increasingly difficult and dangerous. As the US shipped its New World treasures to the beleaguered Napoleonic France, Great Britain intercepted one ship after another, searching and seizing many American vessels. To make matters worse, the British Army had been decimated by decades of war, and so they had grown desperate for new soldiers. Accordingly, they used a barbaric system called "impressment," in which US sailors were violently forced to join Britain's Royal Navy.

With tensions on the rise, US President Thomas Jefferson was desperate to prevent United States citizens from being forced into the service of the nation that his people had fought so hard to escape from. However, his next move would only make matters worse. He placed an embargo on trade with all foreign nations, effectively cutting off the United States from Europe. Although the fledgling nation had proven itself mighty in warfare, it was not yet ready to be totally cut off from the Old World. The American economy crashed, and morale plummeted across the nation.

And while the British were no longer actually present in the US, they were still able to make life hard for the colonists by reaching out to the colonists' greatest enemies: the Native Americans. While amicable relations were possible between the native tribes and the European Americans, Native Americans still had very good reason to fear and despise their colonial counterparts. In their eyes, while these so-called "Americans" had fought for independence, little had changed for the Native Americans themselves. They were still foreigners when compared to the Native Americans, who had been living in that land for untold centuries. Accordingly, when the British began to encourage Native Americans to resist westward expansion, they were only too happy to comply.

Although the ensuing war was called the "War of 1812," it actually lasted for more than two years, and its first battle was fought in 1811. The Battle of Tippecanoe was a clash between American colonists and Native American tribes. Numerous tribes had formed a confederacy in a bid to stand against the Americans, whom they still viewed as invaders on their ancestral land. This confederacy was ruled by the powerful war chief Tecumseh, who was encouraged by his brother Tenskwatawa (a holy man). As much as Tecumseh was determined to win security for his people, his determination couldn't stand against American might. The battle ended badly for Tecumseh.

With thousands of his people dead, the proud warrior chief realized that he couldn't beat the Americans alone. He turned to the British for help, and the Americans realized that the Native American threat was a far greater one than they had first expected. They declared war on the British in 1812. The declaration was signed by President James Madison.

Despite the fact the Americans were massively outnumbered compared to the combined power of the British and Native Americans, the first eighteen months of the war went very well for the Americans. Although their invasion of Canada was a failure, numerous battles within the US itself were fought against Tecumseh and his British allies, many of them ending in American victories. Tecumseh himself was killed in 1813, and while the Native Americans were still involved in the war, his brilliant leadership left a gap in their command. In fact, America was preparing to win its second war against its ancient motherland when everything changed.

Prior to 1814, the war in the New World was very much a secondary concern to the British Crown. Fighting Napoleon was far more pressing than dealing with a bunch of Americans— at least at first. But in 1814, when Napoleon was sent into exile, Britain had men, money, and attention to spare, and it set its sights on America. Perhaps at the time, Britain still saw the Americans as a bunch of rebellious colonists who needed to be taught a lesson. Either way, the British were done playing around, and they threw everything they had at the US.

At first, the result was absolutely devastating. The Battle of Prairie du Chien, fought in the summer of 1814, was one of many defeats. Not even the remote territory of Wisconsin was exempt from the violence that spread all over the country. Only a few weeks after Fort Shelby fell and burned, Washington, DC, was invaded by the British, and the White House burned to the ground.

The burning of the White House incensed the Americans. Their presidency was their pride, their symbol of being a new and progressive nation the likes of which the world had never seen before, as it was one of the earliest democracies in a world still very much ruled by kings and queens. On September 11th, 1814, the naval Battle of Plattsburgh ended, and it was the first great American victory of that year. In Baltimore, Fort McHenry was pounded relentlessly by the British, with shells thundering into its walls for twenty-five hours on September 13th. The fort held, and the British were forced to retreat with their tails between their legs. In celebration, the American soldiers had a massive flag hoisted over their wrecked but undefeated fort. The sight was so emotional for Francis Scott Key that it inspired him to write a poem. It eventually became America's national anthem, "The Star-Spangled Banner."

As for Lieutenant Perkins and the rest of the sixty brave Americans who had manned Fort Shelby against the odds for so long, while their battle ended in defeat, at least their lives were all spared. With his well gone dry and his fort afire, Perkins surrendered to McKay, and he and all of his men were escorted back to St. Louis unmolested.

Luckily for Perkins and his fellow residents of Wisconsin, the War of 1812 ended better than the Battle of Prairie du Chien. By the end of 1814, it was clear that the British weren't going to win, but American resources were also wearing very thin. Both nations had grown tired and were spent by the war. With a stalemate reached across North America, the Treaty of Ghent was signed on Christmas Eve, 1814. Impressment and the trade embargoes had long since ended, but America returned Canada back to British control.

The treaty had already been signed, but the last shot had not yet been fired. News could only travel from Europe to America as fast as a ship could sail, meaning that it would take weeks for the fighting men in America to realize that a treaty had been signed at all. Accordingly, the war officially ended when General Andrew Jackson—who would later become president—defended New Orleans against the British, winning a brilliant but ultimately meaningless victory.

The terms of the treaty were supposed to return everything to the way it had been before the war. However, while territories were returned to their respective owners, there was no changing the fact that America had once again stood up to the might of the British Empire. Even though the War of 1812 had cost America 15,000 lives, it boosted morale hugely among the Americans, who had now defended their budding nation against the greatest power in the world at that time. Relations between America and Europe improved hugely. American ships could trade unmolested with France, and trade even started up again with Britain itself.

Today, the US generally remembers the War of 1812 as a positive thing. However, for the Native Americans, it was a shattering loss that led to tragedy, loss of millions of acres of ancestral land, rampant disease, and even genocide. The British had been the Native Americans' only hope to stop the relentless westward expansion that was slowly eating away at the lands they had roamed for centuries—that was assuming that the British Crown would have kept its promises to the Native Americans, who died in the hundreds during the War of 1812. Although there were many courageous battles against the oncoming tide of settlers, without their British allies, the Native Americans never stood a chance. Tens of thousands of them would be butchered and infected with European diseases.

For Wisconsin itself, the War of 1812 marked the beginning of a new era. Wisconsin was no longer some remote territory barely worth thinking about, as it had been during the American Revolutionary War. Wisconsin had now become something that the US wanted to defend, to build up, and to exploit. Its wilderness was covered in settlements. They might have begun as pioneer villages, but they eventually grew into large communities, towns, and even bustling cities. And while the Battle of Prairie du Chien, Wisconsin's first major battle, was ultimately a defeat, it did call attention to the fact that the territory's defenses were woefully inadequate. Fort Crawford was built in Prairie du Chien on the blackened ruins of Fort Shelby in 1816. Green Bay was also given a large fort of its own, which was named Fort Howard.

The Winnebago War

With independence from Great Britain being thoroughly established, and the United States placed firmly on the map as a formidable nation in its own right, the burgeoning population of the United States began to focus on what would be its major concern for the next century: expansion. In the eyes of the white settlers, the majority of American territory had not yet been explored, and its untapped resources were bursting with potential. The growing population began to expand across the United States, including Wisconsin. But wherever they went, they found something that could be either an annoyance or a major obstacle: the native peoples.

The failure of Tecumseh's uprising had by no means brought an end to the conflict between the Native Americans and pioneers. Wherever there was a frontier, there were huge communities of people who were viewed as being somehow undeserving of the land and liberties that Americans prized so highly, thanks to the racism that was so fundamental to 19th-century thinking. Wisconsin was no exception.

The Winnebago War was not so much a real war as an isolated uprising in what was then the Michigan Territory, but it was a dark portent of what was still to come. The Winnebago, or Ho-Chunk, had had largely peaceful relations with settlers for centuries, ever since Jean Nicolet first made contact with them in the 16th century with his extravagant robes and gentle manner. However, as Wisconsin grew more and more crowded with settlers, things began to sour between the Ho-Chunk and the Americans. Trade was still active, and the tensions simmered below the surface for the most part. Most settlers believed that the Native Americans could be "civilized," which meant they believed the tribes could be assimilated into Western society.

However, many Ho-Chunk saw no reason why they should change everything they knew and held dear just for the sake of a bunch of settlers. Some of them even considered a violent solution, although, to all appearances, this was an isolated minority. Nonetheless, this minority could be extremely dangerous.

This became evident in March 1826. A small mixed-race family—part Native American, part European—was harvesting maple syrup near Prairie du Chien when they were brutally murdered in cold blood. Apparently, a Ho-Chunk raiding party had done the ugly deed, and the US military cracked down on them immediately. Two men were arrested for the murder, but they escaped not long afterward.

In response, the incensed US Army, determined to gain justice for the murdered family, captured two innocent Ho-Chunk and held them hostage. They wouldn't be released until the killers were brought to justice. The tribe cooperated quickly, and in accordance with their ancient tribal traditions, they brought six Ho-Chunk to Fort Crawford that summer. Unfortunately, most of these men were not actually involved in the murder; the Ho-Chunk saw them as sacrifices, scapegoats to secure the liberty of the hostages who'd been imprisoned in Fort Crawford for weeks. This angered the Americans even more. They demanded the actual murderers be brought to them, and eventually, Waukookah and Mahnaatapakah were brought to Fort Crawford. They were identified as the men who'd murdered the small family at Prairie du Chien.

The two men were indicted shortly afterward, and the hostages were returned to the Ho-Chunk tribe. That could have very well been the end of it. It was clear that the Ho-Chunk were ready for peace and that the murder of the family had been an isolated incident. Unfortunately, the two murderers didn't stay at Fort Crawford for long. They were sent to Fort Snelling instead, and while the Ho-Chunk had been under the impression that the killers would be imprisoned instead of executed, rumors rapidly began to circulate that Waukookah and Mahnaatapakah had been killed. Matters were made far worse when more rumors began to flood the Ho-Chunk circles, telling of a group of sailors who'd disembarked from an American keelboat to capture and rape a group of innocent young Ho-Chunk women.

These rumors could not have possibly come at a worse time. Americans had discovered lead in Wisconsin. This was many years before anyone was aware that lead could be poisonous, and the metal was used to make everything from bullets to pencils to paint. The whole world was hungry for lead, and when Americans learned that Wisconsin's forests hid abundant amounts of the metal, they flocked to the territory to mine it. These desperate pioneers had little regard for whose land they were mining on. They'd been encroaching illegally on Ho-Chunk land for years, and the US military was more than happy to look the other way. Even those who hoped to "civilize" the Ho-Chunk still saw them as being inferior creatures thanks to their native heritage.

Throughout the fall and winter, these damaging rumors and very real issues wore away at the Ho-Chunks' relationship with the

Americans. They refused to attend gatherings or meetings. As a result, diplomatic relations were effectively cut off, and the uprising itself would begin in June 1827.

Red Bird was a Ho-Chunk leader who had had enough. His land was being taken from him, his people were being oppressed, and he had reached the end of his tether. Something snapped in him that summer—something dark and awful that inspired appalling violence. He had to take it out on someone, to get revenge for all that had been done to his people. And so, with two associates, he headed down to the home of Registre Gagnier, ostensibly to seek peace but, in reality, to seek revenge.

Gagnier had a family friend with him at the time, and he lived in a small cabin with his wife, son, and baby girl. He was one of the few settlers who were ready to hear the Ho-Chunks' concerns, so he willingly invited Red Bird into his home with the two other Ho-Chunk. For Gagnier, his faith in the Ho-Chunk would end in tragedy.

It's uncertain what exactly happened in that cabin on that awful day, who it was that did the killing, or whether Red Bird's associates knew what he'd been planning. Either way, within minutes, Gagnier and his friend were both dead, shot and killed by the Ho-Chunk. They turned on Mrs. Gagnier next, ready to sink a lead bullet into her flesh, but she'd been raising a family on the American frontier for years. She was as tough as they came, and she managed to wrestle the gun away from one of the Ho-Chunk, grab her young son, and flee into the woods. Tragically, she had not been able to get to her baby girl. The screaming child was stabbed and scalped alive.

With the scalps of Gagnier, his friend, and the baby in hand—her tiny scalp almost hairless—Red Bird and his friends returned to his village at Prairie La Crosse, where the sight inspired several of his villagers to join his rebellion. Bolstered by the ease with which he'd massacred Gagnier, Red Bird was ready and hungry for more American blood. With a growing number of angry supporters, he turned on the keelboats that traveled up and down the Mississippi

River, launching an attack that would end in the deaths of two Americans and seven Ho-Chunk.

Fear grew thick among the settlers as they realized how awfully outnumbered they were by the Native Americans who surrounded them. The arrogance they'd found so palatable in thinking they could assimilate the Native Americans into their lifestyle had turned into a bitter draft of terror, and the settlers prepared for war. So did Red Bird. He wanted revenge, and he wanted the Americans gone. He started contacting other tribes in Wisconsin, but to his surprise, he found limited success. Despite the pressing issues the settlers had caused, most Native American tribes had no interest whatsoever in warfare. Only a few Potawatomi were convinced to join the uprising by attacking and killing some livestock that belonged to the settlers. However, at the urging of other tribes, the Potawatomi gave it up. Even the other Ho-Chunk—those who didn't live in Red Bird's village—refused to be a part of his uprising.

Still, the US Army was intimidated by the violence that Red Bird and his band had shown. A new fort was built, and as the summer wore on, more and more US troops filed into Wisconsin, filling Forts Crawford and Howard with American soldiers and their Native American allies, who had sided with the settlers in the hopes of securing peace quickly. No attacks were launched, but the looming threat of the US Army was more than enough to cow Red Bird. He realized what he was up against and that he was largely alone in his thirst for war, and no further action was taken.

On the contrary, frightened by the possibility of war, the Ho-Chunk had decided to cooperate with the military once again. They eventually turned Red Bird and his associates over to the US Army. While many of the Ho-Chunk were completely pardoned and allowed to return to their people, Red Bird himself would not be so lucky. He was imprisoned for several months before contracting dysentery and dying behind bars.

The Black Hawk War

The thought of "civilizing" Native Americans had been popular among Wisconsin's settlers for years, but the Winnebago War had changed that radically. The awful violence of Red Bird's attack on the Gagnier family had left the settlers shaken, their confidence in Native Americans destroyed. Many of them now turned to thinking that Native Americans had to be uprooted from Wisconsin completely and expelled westward.

Only five years after the Winnebago War, a second uprising broke out, making the settlers' relations with Native Americans even worse. This time, it was the once-friendly Sauk who would rise up in protest of the Americans' constant encroachment on the land their tribe had lived on for thousands of years, perhaps ever since the Boaz mastodon was killed with a Clovis spearhead.

The leader of this rebellion was named Black Hawk. Born in 1767, he lived in Saukenuk, the very same village where the traumatized, injured, and bedraggled remnants of the Meskwaki tribe had fled after the Fox Wars had ripped them to pieces. Now, the Fox and the Sauk had grown together, and Saukenuk was an important part of their society. Unfortunately, it was also in danger of being completely taken over by American settlers. Regardless of the fact that the Sauk had been living there for hundreds of years, settlers believed they had more of a right to the lead-rich land than its native inhabitants and demanded ownership of it. In 1804, the Sauk and other tribes had officially ceded their land to the Americans, hoping to avoid a conflict. At first, this seemed to have worked, as American settlers didn't come to Saukenuk for decades.

Eventually, though, Americans' insatiable appetite for land had gobbled up every scrap of dirt all the way to Saukenuk itself. Black Hawk had once looked out on an untouched wilderness from his village. Now, there were settlers everywhere, and they were starting to demand that Black Hawk take his people and leave. Although he had legally ceded his land to the Americans, this last injustice riled Black Hawk beyond description. He dug in and refused to go.

Knowing that refusing land to the Americans was as good as a declaration of war, Black Hawk began to gather support from other tribes. He was a well-respected man, more so than Red Bird, and the other tribes were beginning to grow more desperate. Black Hawk was also quick to single out tribes that he knew would fight the Americans. He had the Sauk, and he also approached the Meskwaki and Kickapoo tribes, both of whom had fought on the British side during the American Revolutionary War and the War of 1812. In a matter of weeks, Black Hawk had amassed a considerable army, constituting a far larger threat to the settlers of Wisconsin than Red Bird's scattered rebellion.

The US Army was once again quick to respond. A militia was gathered and placed under the command of General Edmund P. Gaines, who was determined to teach the Native Americans a lesson about giving American pioneers the land they so desired. Daunted by the size of the militia, Black Hawk returned to his own side of the Mississippi, hiding out for a short while as he prepared his troops. He wouldn't stay away for long, though. On April 5th, 1832, he crossed the Mississippi again and faced Gaines's army in the first spate of violence of the Black Hawk War.

It didn't take long for Black Hawk to realize that he was in far over his head. Like other leaders before him, Black Hawk had underestimated the sheer size of the US Army, and during the battle, he realized that this fight would be a futile one. He attempted to surrender, but confusion still reigned. With the soldiers' blood still burning with battle, an American soldier shot and killed one of Black Hawk's men. The battle began anew once more, and the Black Hawk War had officially begun.

Despite Black Hawk's misgivings, it started out well for the Native Americans. The following month, Black Hawk clashed again with the US Army, and this time, he won a powerful victory that left the

Americans licking their wounds. Bolstered by this victory, Black Hawk and his troops held out for the summer, keeping the Americans off their land until a terrible battle practically annihilated the Native Americans on August 2nd. Black Hawk was given no choice but to surrender. He had lost around 600 men, while only 70 Americans were killed.

For Black Hawk, a proud warrior who had done his best to protect his land and people, the story ends in terrible humiliation. Not only was Saukenuk taken by the Americans, but Black Hawk himself was thrown into chains, then dragged all over the United States territories as a kind of trophy of war. Beaten, pushed around, his hands bound, angry and helpless, Black Hawk was shown off to other Native Americans to show them how useless it would be to stage an uprising. From one town to the next, Black Hawk was forced to watch hope die in the eyes of the Native Americans.

His death was a peaceful one, but it was nonetheless humiliating. Black Hawk would live out the rest of his days under the supervision of a fellow Sauk leader who had long been one of his enemies, dying a natural death.

The Milwaukee Bridge War

By the mid-19th century, Wisconsin had been intermittently involved in one war or another for almost a hundred years. From the hard-fought American Revolution to the bitter War of 1812, the bloody Winnebago War and the disastrous Black Hawk War, Wisconsin had seen years of deadly conflict. But the next war to take place in this territory was far less deadly—and its source was a unique and amusing one.

With the Native Americans now out of the way, Wisconsin was safe enough for settlers to come pouring in. These were courageous but often penniless young men who were ready to seek their fortunes. There had already been around 4,000 lead miners in Wisconsin before the Winnebago War. Now that there was no competition for the land, settlers came flooding in to mine Wisconsin's lead-rich earth. While some of these miners were American, many were immigrants from the Old World. In the early days, many came from Cornwall. Later, German and Scandinavian immigrants would become commonplace in Wisconsin.

Although these prospectors were flooding into Wisconsin for a much less romantic metal than gold, the effect on the state was not unlike a miniature version of California's Gold Rush. Boomtowns began to spring up across Wisconsin; names like "New Diggings" point to these towns' origins as lead mining towns. Soon, Wisconsin was no longer some far-flung colony that no one much cared about.

The miners who produced its lead, just like the gold prospectors in the West, were often impoverished men who had spent their last penny to move to Wisconsin. They lived in ramshackle shelters during the summer, constantly working the earth. When winter came, they seldom had the means to build cabins in which to live. Instead, they hollowed out burrows in the frozen earth of the hills, seeking shelter from the elements in these holes in the ground, much like badgers. For this reason, Wisconsin was nicknamed the "Badger State," and it remains its nickname to this day.

By 1836, Wisconsin was producing half the United States' lead. On April 20th of that year, it was made a formal territory with a governor, with the first being Henry Dodge. At the time, though, the Wisconsin Territory was very different than the Wisconsin State we know today. For one thing, it was enormous; it contained modern-day Wisconsin, Minnesota, Iowa, and much of North and South Dakota.

Belmont, today a tiny village, was the first capital of Wisconsin. Today, its population numbers only around 1,000 people; back then, it was even smaller, and it quickly proved insufficient to be the capital city of such a truly vast territory. Instead, a new city was constructed on the shores of Lake Michigan. It was named Madison after the US president. Madison remains the capital of Wisconsin to this day.

Even then—and to this day—Madison wasn't the biggest city in Wisconsin. That honor belongs to Milwaukee. Today, Milwaukee is the fifth-largest city in the Midwest, but it has been a human settlement for longer than we really know—perhaps even longer than the Ho-Chunk and Menominee tribes have existed. Their ancestors likely settled the site for the first time many years before Christopher Columbus ever set sail.

In the late 18th century, a Frenchman built a trading post at Milwaukee and spent time there among the Ho-Chunk who had made it their home. It was inevitably overrun by Americans in the next fifty years, and it became some of Wisconsin's most promising real estate, thanks to its location on Lake Michigan.

It wasn't long before three Americans realized how much promise the Milwaukee area held. Since it was largely undeveloped at the time, it was perfect for building houses and businesses, and these three men quickly bought up parcels of land right next to one another. These men were Byron Kilbourn, Solomon Juneau, and George Walker—the fathers of Milwaukee.

Building their open patches of bare land into something more wasn't difficult. In fact, buildings sprang up so quickly that it wasn't long before each parcel of land was so built-up that the sections looked like a single town. There were just two barriers between the sections: the Milwaukee River and the residents' rivalry with one another.

"Milwaukee" was not yet a city. In fact, the west and east sides of the city, which were separated by the river, were called Juneautown and Kilbourntown after their founders, and these two men were engaged in a stubborn rivalry. (George Walker, whose town was named Walker's Point, was less involved in the conflict.) Kilbourntown on the west was larger and more prosperous; Byron Kilbourn did his best to keep things that way, alienating the east side. Meanwhile, Juneautown on the east was stubbornly refusing to back down and acknowledge Kilbourntown's superiority. A similar resentment brewed among the residents; the west side residents considered themselves to be far superior to the rabble on the east, who thought that the west siders were arrogant snobs.

Nonetheless, even though the residents wanted little to do with each other, they still needed each other. The two towns were not independent of one another, no matter how much they wanted to be. The residents had to cross back and forth across the river to get to businesses, churches, and post offices. As a result, building a bridge across the Milwaukee River was necessary. However, Kilbourn and Juneau both stubbornly refused to be the one to link their two towns; they were determined to cling to their perceived independence. So, a weary ferry crossed back and forth a few times a day, resulting in long and frustrating waits for the citizens, who sometimes couldn't cross over at all when there wasn't any space on the ferry.

Eventually, when it became clear that neither of the men was going to grow up and work together, the county commissioners got involved. A bridge was funded and built in 1840, but building it was no easy feat. Because Juneau and Kilbourn were rivals, they had never dreamed that their two towns could someday be linked, so the streets of the towns didn't line up. The bridge had to be built at an angle across the river so that it would connect Division and Chestnut Streets.

The bridge was a thorn in Kilbourn's side, but for the residents, it was heaven-sent. At last, they could simply walk or drive their carriages across a bridge if they wished to go to the other side of town. The improvement was so great that residents began to fund and build their own bridges in other parts of Milwaukee. Although this did make travel much easier, some of the west side residents, spurred on by Kilbourn, were deeply unhappy about this bridge. To make matters worse, although the Chestnut Street bridge was a drawbridge to allow for ships to pass down the Milwaukee and into the lake, Kilbourn bitterly claimed that the bridge interfered with shipping traffic, most of which was headed toward his ports in Lake Michigan.

The bridge had been standing for five years when things came to a head. A schooner ran into one of the bridges over the Milwaukee, and the west side residents, who were still paying a raised tax for the construction of the Chestnut Street bridge, were outraged at the prospect of paying even more taxes to repair the bridge. On May 8th, 1845, they formed an angry mob and stormed the Chestnut Street bridge, tearing down the west side of it and sending their own tax dollars splashing into the foaming water of the Milwaukee.

The conflict was nicknamed the Bridge War. "War" is a little hyperbole; there were some injuries and much damage done to property, but no one was killed in the conflict. Still, violence was rampant in the streets, as citizens of Kilbourntown and Juneautown tore down bridges. Juneautown's residents even stuffed a cannon full of clock weights and threatened to fire it on Kilbourn's home.

Riots and spates of violence, as well as the demolition of bridges, would continue for several months and deep into the winter. While some of the bridges were eventually rebuilt, as the people realized they needed the bridges after all, there was no real resolution until January 1846 when Kilbourntown, Juneautown, and Walker's Point were officially unified into the single city of Milwaukee.

Evidence of the Milwaukee Bridge War still remains to this day. While the unified city prospered and has grown into the biggest city in Wisconsin, the streets of downtown Milwaukee still don't line up. Its bridges across the river are still built at angles thanks to the petty squabbles of its obstinate early residents.

Approaching Statehood

By the end of the Milwaukee Bridge War, Wisconsin was a very different place than it had been at the end of British colonization. It had become a territory of a free America. It had seen its first major battle during the War of 1812, and it had been the setting for two bitter conflicts between Native Americans and white settlers. Its settlers had even had their first squabble among themselves. Wisconsin had gone from being home to a handful of trappers, miners, and brave pioneers to being a territory filled with towns and cities, producing a vast quantity of lead.

Wisconsin had seen plenty of conflict since the American Revolution. But it was about to face the most bitter conflict of them all: the American Civil War.

Chapter 5 – Wisconsin as a State

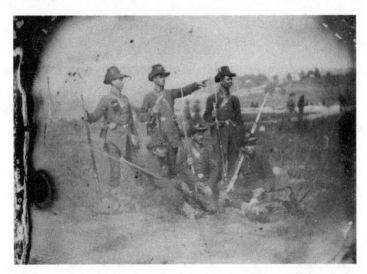

Illustration III: Wisconsinite soldiers of the Iron Brigade in the American Civil War

By the time of the Milwaukee Bridge War, Wisconsin's population had grown to 150,000 residents. Its booming lead mining industry and growing agricultural sector was supporting a vibrant community, yet it was still not an official state.

With the Milwaukee Bridge War out of the way, by the beginning of 1846, citizens were determined to change that. A convention was held and a document drafted that year. Its ideas were hugely progressive for the time; it suggested the possibility of allowing people of color to vote. This idea was too extreme even for the free-thinking Wisconsinites, though, and another document was drawn up the following year that soothed the more conservative citizens enough for them to vote it into statehood on May 29th, 1848. Wisconsin became the 30th state.

Wisconsin had been presided over by a governor since its admittance into the US as a territory twelve years earlier. The year it became a state, a new governor had to be elected, and he would have to be a notable man to change Wisconsin's politics from that of a territory to a state. At the time, the US had two major political parties: the Democrats and the Whigs. The first governor of Wisconsin State was a Democrat, and his name was Nelson Dewey.

Governor Nelson Dewey

Dewey was born in Connecticut and studied in New York State at Hamilton Academy before he moved to Cassville, Wisconsin, a small village where he practiced law. It was through his work as an attorney that Dewey was elected to his first political position: the Register of Deeds in his local county, Grant County. At the time, Henry Dodge was still the governor of the Wisconsin Territory, and he met Dewey while the latter was the Register of Deeds. The young man's diligence and intellect impressed Dodge, who helped him to his role of the Justice of the Peace in 1838.

Over the next ten years, Dewey would continue to expand his political career and his personal wealth. He became the district attorney of Grant County and served on the territorial council for a period. He also began to invest in the lead mines that had put Wisconsin on the map, as well as buying up large parts of land in and around his village until he owned most of Cassville. It would appear that he was a likable landlord. When he joined the Democratic Party shortly before Wisconsin became a state, he was rapidly elected to become its leader. He beat the Whig candidate to become the first governor of Wisconsin at the age of thirty-five.

Many of Dewey's views would shape Wisconsin's politics in the decades to come, including its role in the Civil War. Although the Democratic Party of the time was not always against slavery, Dewey was a devoted abolitionist. While many of the Southern states were clinging to their right to keep, sell, and abuse human beings, Dewey refused to permit slavery in his state, and he also spoke out against slavery being allowed in any of the new states that were rapidly joining the US during this time of constant westward expansion. As a state, Wisconsin would never see its African American residents in chains. Dewey also made its transition into statehood a smooth one, and Wisconsin prospered under his leadership.

Tragically, Dewey's personal story does not end well. After his term as governor was over, he never found political success again, even though he ran for a number of positions in the following years. His family life also took a turn for the worse; one of his three children died young, and his wife left him with the other two, eventually going all the way to Europe—she never saw Dewey again. He even lost all of his wealth in the Panic of 1873 and died alone and penniless in the village he'd once owned.

The Escape of Joshua Glover

Dewey's beliefs as an abolitionist made Wisconsin an important state for enslaved people who were seeking to escape their harsh chains. Missouri, then the northernmost slave state, was separated from Wisconsin only by Iowa, making it possible for Missourian slaves to flee to safety in Wisconsin. Many would cross through Wisconsin in their bid to reach free Canada.

Nonetheless, two years after Wisconsin became a state, most of its population, which had doubled in just five years, was composed of Yankees from the Northeast United States, German immigrants, and British immigrants, although there were also over 60,000 native-born Wisconsinites. Despite the fact that Wisconsin's statehood had coincided with a decline in lead mining, its agriculture and logging industries were growing at a rate that supported its booming population with ease, in large part thanks to railroads that had been extended from Chicago, Illinois, into Wisconsin by 1850. This made it much easier for goods to be exported to the rest of the US, resulting in such a large boom of industries that by 1854 the railroad had reached Madison. Soon, Wisconsin's entire state was served by a network of steam trains.

Another railroad—this one figurative—was also stretching across Wisconsin around this time. Although Wisconsin, as well as most of the Northern United States, did not allow slavery, the entire United States still fell under the barbaric Fugitive Slave Act. This act had snuffed out hope for many slaves who had just had a taste of freedom, for it ruled that escaped slaves could be captured and returned to their owners even if they managed to reach a free state. "Slave catchers," people who tracked escaped slaves to the free states, very often captured them on the very threshold of their liberty, dragging them back to a harsh and abusive life. Abolitionists were fighting this act, but in the meantime, they had to figure out a way to help slaves escape to true freedom: Canada. No slave catcher could follow them there.

To this end, abolitionist movements established a network of homes across the Northern states where escaped slaves could be offered shelter and safety from slave catchers, allowing them to move across the states to Canada in comparative safety. This network was nicknamed the "Underground Railroad," even though no actual trains were involved. One of the most important abolitionists in Wisconsin was Sherman Booth, a leader of the Underground Railroad in the state. He also published the *Wisconsin Freeman*, an abolitionist newspaper. He assisted many slaves through the Underground Railroad to freedom.

Not all escaped slaves merely passed through Wisconsin. In fact, many escapees found Wisconsin's communities so pleasant that they risked capture to live out their lives among its forests and lakes, easily finding work in its burgeoning industries. One such man was named Joshua Glover.

Little is known about Joshua's early life. Like most slaves, he was not considered to be a human being, and only rudimentary records were kept of his existence before his escape. It was also absolutely forbidden for slaves to ever learn to read or write; in fact, many, like Joshua, didn't know their own birthdays, so no one knows exactly when Joshua was born. History's best guess is between 1810 and 1830.

While Joshua's ancestors had been born in Africa and were shipped across the Atlantic Ocean in the most brutal conditions imaginable, Joshua himself was born in the US to two slave parents. It's unclear whether his parents were in love or whether he was "bred"—meaning his parents were forced to have children as if they were nothing more than pigs or cattle. He would have grown up in worse conditions than most farmers keep their livestock. Sleeping in a filthy, communal hovel at night, Joshua's mother was likely forced to work throughout her pregnancy and even when she was nursing her infant. If she failed to keep up the pace, she would have been physically punished, perhaps by a brutal whipping.

Since he was born to a slave, Joshua was automatically a slave himself, making him the property of his mother's owner. When his owner's children were playing with toys, riding their ponies, and going to school, Joshua was learning work routines and helping his mother with her duties. This happened as early as the age of four. Playtime was scarce; in a bid to keep their slaves subdued and less likely to escape or rebel, many owners only allowed them three or four hours of sleep each night and even less time to themselves. By the time he was eight or ten, Joshua would be put to work on his own, and he stood the chance of being sold right out of his mother's arms. Any attempt to resist would be met with severe physical punishment. He would be forced to do all kinds of menial duties depending on his owner's will; boys often worked in the fields, but they could also be employed in the kitchens or gardens. Slaves were never even taught to speak proper English. Despite the fact that English was their first and usually only language, their grammar and pronunciation were habitually poor. Slave owners liked it that way. It made them sound stupid and inferior to the academically educated ears of those who lacked enough humanity to recognize that the men and women they owned, sold, bought, and abused were people just like them.

We don't know when exactly Joshua was sold by his original owner or how many owners he went through before history finds him for the first time in 1850. Aged somewhere between twenty and forty, Joshua was sold to the last owner he'd ever have on January 1st. This man, Benammi Stone Garland, was a resident of St. Louis, Missouri. At the time, slave and free states were separated by geography; the Missouri Compromise was named after slavery's northernmost state. The states south of Missouri kept slaves, while the states north of it didn't. At St. Louis, Joshua found himself on the very edge of the enslaved world, just a few miles away from Illinois. While Illinois had harsh and racist laws, it was still a free state. Right across that border, men and women with brown skins were living free lives while Joshua labored under Garland's oppression. He was chopping wood, hauling water, and mucking stalls for no pay when his counterparts just across the border were getting married, working jobs, and learning to read.

For two years, Joshua did the most menial tasks for Garland, suffering punishments and facing one long, meaningless day after the other. Finally, in 1852, he could take it no longer. He escaped to Illinois on foot and penniless, with nothing but hope and courage to bear him onward. It took him weeks to trek through the state afoot until he finally reached the town of Racine, Wisconsin, which is close to Milwaukee.

Wisconsin wasn't Canada, but Joshua instantly liked it there. It felt far enough from Missouri, and this free state seemed like a different world. While African Americans were not yet allowed to vote in Wisconsin, it still had some of the most progressive laws in the US, and Joshua found a free and happy life there. He easily found employment and settled down in a home in Racine, where he lived for two happy years, making friends and finally living the dream of being a free man.

But Joshua wasn't a free man. No escaped slave in the United States could ever be truly free, not while the Fugitive Slave Act still existed. Despite Wisconsin's surging abolitionist movement and its strong political ideologies about freedom, there was nothing that Wisconsinites could do if an escaped slave was arrested and dragged back to a life of bondage. At least, there used to be nothing until March 1854 made the story of Joshua Glover a famous one.

Joshua was at his home, visiting with a pair of friends, on a beautiful spring evening in the little town. What he didn't know, however, was that one of his so-called friends was nothing but a traitor. Perhaps bribed with money or driven by racism (history is unclear on this "friend's" identity), this man had told slave catchers where Joshua could be found. And even as Joshua talked and laughed in his own home, his old owner was creeping nearer, backed up by seven others, including a marshal and numerous slave catchers. These men caught and subdued free people for a living. Joshua was just another paycheck to them.

They burst into his home, subdued his true friend, and attacked Joshua. Before Joshua really knew what was happening, a wooden club was smacked into his skull, throwing him to the ground. The dread coldness of steel manacles was thrown around his wrists. The feeling filled him with an old terror, with decades of trauma that drove him to his feet. He fought to break free, to rush out of the door and into the darkness that could save him. But it was an unfair fight, eight against one. The men fell upon him with fists and feet, and Joshua was beaten senseless.

When Joshua woke, he was behind bars once more, languishing in Milwaukee's jail. It was a dark night, and the next morning, Garland would drag him back to his old life in St. Louis—a life without friends, without love, without rights, without a voice. That cold night in jail must have been unimaginably terrible for a man who'd drunk so deeply of the cup of freedom only to have that life-giving liquid wrenched so cruelly from his desperate hands.

But it was not to be. The people of Racine had gotten wind of Joshua's kidnapping, and within the night, they were up in arms. Joshua was a well-respected member of their community; he was a friend, a fellow citizen, a Wisconsinite. And Racine's people were not about to let him be treated like some wayward livestock. Joshua's friend had told them all about the brutal beating that the poor man had endured already. Racine's residents believed in freedom, and they had had enough.

It wasn't long before Sherman Booth found out what had happened, and his blood was on fire to set Joshua free. Seizing a horse, Sherman raced across the local towns, calling Racine and Milwaukee to arms. And while Sherman knew that the law was not on Joshua's side, something more powerful than the law was at play: the voice of the people.

When Garland woke the next morning, it was to a breathtaking spectacle. The people of Racine and Milwaukee had rallied, and thousands of them—about 5,000 by some estimates, which was one-quarter of Milwaukee's population at the time—had gathered in front of the jail where Joshua was being kept. Their protests had become a riot in the streets. Waves of anger, noise, and discontent pounded against the walls, and from where he was huddled in a darkened cell, Joshua could hear the roar of his supporters from the street outside. There was the crack and snap of bonfires burning, casting some of their yellow glow into his prison; cannons spoke, their booms shaking the floor; snatches of music reached him, and it gave him a taste of the hope that had borne him all the way from St. Louis to Racine in the first place.

Such were the protests that eventually a court order was signed to have Joshua set free. However, the sheriff presiding over the jail was aware that these were legally muddy waters. He refused to let Joshua go, and Sherman took matters into his own hands. He knew that the protesters were fired up and that they more than outnumbered Milwaukee's authorities. After rallying them, he stormed into the jail.

In moments, Joshua had an army of people in the jail with him. In a few moments more, they'd torn down the door and borne him out into the daylight. A horse and buggy were waiting to take Joshua to freedom, and the exhausted, wounded man was tucked safely into the buggy and driven away from town in short order. Joshua Glover was free at last.

Joshua would live out the rest of his life in relative obscurity. The Underground Railroad brought him safely to Canada, where he lived out his years in freedom. But his name remained on the lips of Wisconsinites, and it rang with indignation. The fact that a member of a Wisconsin community was nearly dragged off into slavery was an intolerable one for many, and it pushed rising discontent about the Fugitive Slave Act over the brink. Wisconsin's Supreme Court declared the Fugitive Slave Act illegal shortly after the Joshua Glover incident. While the US Supreme Court overturned this ruling, Wisconsin pushed back, making it illegal for any escaped slaves to be captured in the state.

This division was being echoed all over the United States during the 1850s. One free state after another was pushing back against the Fugitive Slave Act and against slavery as a whole. Abolitionist movements were gaining power, and in Wisconsin, the first abolitionist political party was born only months after Joshua's escape.

The Birth of the Republican Party

In the 1850s, tensions regarding slavery had been rising for decades, and they were on the brink of eruption. The first crack in the surface came in 1854. Westward expansion had claimed vast tracts of territory in the American West, extending the United States all the way to its western shoreline. Mining shanties were being replaced by homesteads, and the era of the Old West was under way, with pioneers giving way to permanent settlers bent on eking out a living in these harsh new lands. And wherever Americans went, the question of slavery went with them.

Abolitionists pushed hard against allowing such a brutal and archaic system to continue in the new states, arguing that all new western states should be free. And at first, this was the case. The Missouri Compromise's geographical distinction worked well. All that changed in 1854 when the Kansas-Nebraska Act allowed settlers to vote on whether or not they wanted slavery to follow them into their states.

It was a massive blow to the abolitionist movement. It was a political disaster even for those who were neutral on the slavery issue. At the time, the balance of power in the United States was distinctly divided along one line: slavery. The free states of the West were naturally more inclined to ally themselves with Northern politicians and ideas, and the advent of slavery in the West could tip the balance of power in favor of the South. Tensions rose, but nowhere as much as in Kansas itself.

Settlers in Kansas felt passionate about the slavery issue just as people did across the country. However, in the rest of the country, there were clear distinctions between slave and free states. Now that Kansas could go either way, its citizens started to fight over the issue, and it wasn't long before the fighting turned physical. By 1856, it was practically a civil war contained within the borders of a single territory, leading to a three-year period of violence known as Bleeding Kansas.

At the time of Bleeding Kansas, there were two major political parties in the United States, but a third was rapidly gaining power. The first was the Democrats (originally the Democratic-Republicans), the second was the Whigs. While some Democrat or Whig leaders could be abolitionists, as was the case with Nelson Dewey, neither party had taken a firm stand on stopping slavery in the westward states. All that changed in a tiny Wisconsin schoolhouse on the precipice of summer in 1854.

Members of the Democrats and Whigs—as well as other more minor political parties in the Union—had grown concerned over the lack of a clear stance on this issue. In fact, many people were convinced that the time was ripe to establish a party that would eventually seek to abolish slavery in its entirety, even in the South. With none of the existing parties ready to make this change, it was decided that a new one would have to be created.

This decision was made by a young lawyer named Alvan Earle Bovay. Like many of Wisconsin's politicians, Alvan had been educated in New York. He'd moved to the small town of Ripon, Wisconsin, where he practiced law and also became a pillar of the community, helping to establish a new college. Alvan was deeply passionate about the issue of slavery, particularly in new territories. Joshua Glover's escape was still making headlines in Wisconsin when the Kansas-Nebraska Act was passed. Like many Wisconsinites, Alvan had been shaken by the Joshua Glover incident, and he couldn't fathom allowing slavery to gain ground. Although he was a Whig at the time, it was clear that the party wasn't doing all that it could to stop the spread of slavery.

So, Alvan decided it was time to take matters into his own hands.

The meeting began on May 20th, 1854. Ripon, still a small town to this day, had few buildings that were suitable for any kind of meeting at all; the school was the one place that Alvan thought he could gather other politicians to discuss the matter. It was no major building with classrooms and halls either. In fact, Ripon's school was a single-roomed schoolhouse, and the concerned citizens had to cram themselves into the tiny building. Despite their cramped quarters, that night, they changed history.

The Republican Party was born in the Little White Schoolhouse that evening, and it took its first breath of air in Wisconsin. These people were ready to change the Union and the world. While its agenda was not strictly abolitionist at first, it was strongly anti-slavery and especially anti-slavery in the new states. Two months later, a large convention was held in Jackson, Michigan, establishing the party. In 1856, as Bleeding Kansas raged in the West, it was a fully-fledged political party, and its candidate had been elected to the role of governor in Wisconsin.

The American Civil War

By 1860, just six years after the Republican Party was established in the first place, the Republicans had become a force to be reckoned with across the Union, so much so that its leader was running for president. Abraham Lincoln, a name now deeply engraved into the very face of history, was elected as president that year. Almost instantly, chaos erupted across the Union. Lincoln was a vociferous and well-known abolitionist who advocated tirelessly against slavery. His election was symbolic of the South's decline in power; few Southern voters would have ever chosen an abolitionist to be their leader, considering how many white Americans (African Americans, of course, had no rights to vote at the time) were deeply dependent on slavery to fuel their businesses and way of life. The election of Lincoln was enough to convince the South that there was no peaceful way to cling to its oppressive ways. Many of the states there revolted against Lincoln's leadership. They refused to be a part of his Union and seceded. The first to go were Georgia, Alabama, South Carolina, Louisiana, and Texas; North Carolina, Arkansas, Tennessee, and Virginia were all too quick to follow. The Union was a union no longer. The United States had been cloven brutally in half.

The seceded states formed an entirely new power, which they named the Confederate States of America, led by President Jefferson Davis. It was clear by this point that there was no way that diplomacy or politics could solve this issue. The violence that had been simmering in Kansas spilled over into the rest of the United States when the Confederacy demanded that Union soldiers remove themselves from its states. The Union refused, and the Confederacy attacked, bombarding Fort Sumter in Charleston Harbor until its soldiers were forced to surrender in March 1861.

When the war began, it would appear that the odds were skewed in favor of the Union, especially considering how much the Confederacy's political power had been decreasing in previous years. However, while it was true that the Union had access to vast resources and a larger population of fighting men, the Confederacy had a simple advantage: training. Generations of Confederates had been officers in the previous wars, and some of America's best commanders and soldiers had come from the South. To add to this, the Confederacy had a small population, but its geographical region was enormous. Conquering such a vast territory under the control of such well-trained men was no mean feat.

Nonetheless, the Union made their first attempt that summer, sending General Winfield Scott and his forces to clash with the famous Confederate general "Stonewall" Jackson near Manassas, Virginia, in the First Battle of Bull Run. The Union troops were beaten and sent scrambling back northward; Scott was rapidly replaced by General George B. McClellan, who had similar luck, fighting one defeat after the other against Stonewall and his colleague, the brilliant yet ill-fated General Robert E. Lee.

By August 1862, the war had been raging for a year. Henry W. Halleck was the third general in command of the Union forces, and the Union's troops were starting to show their lack of experience in command, as the brilliant maneuvers of Lee and Stonewall defeated the Union's greater numbers time after time. The Second Battle of Bull Run was fought that month, and it was an eerie echo of the first, once again sending the Union packing.

The Confederates had started the war on the defensive, but now, they were ready to launch an invasion of their own. Marching on the Union, the Confederates were now planning not only on keeping slavery in their territories but also on expanding their power into the struggling Union. McClellan, who had been replaced as the supreme commander but still had charge over the Union Army of the Potomac, was the unlikely hero who would come to the rescue in this desperate hour. Going directly against orders from Abraham Lincoln himself, McClellan clashed with the Confederates in Maryland, forcing them into Sharpsburg on September 11th. Just two days later, McClellan attacked Lee's encamped troops once again on the banks of the Antietam River. This battle rapidly turned bloody. Men fell left and right, their blood staining the foaming waters. The Battle of Antietam quickly turned into one of the deadliest in the American Civil War. Over 25,000 men died that day, roughly divided equally between the Confederates and the Union. For the Confederacy, it would be a hard defeat; for the Union, it was a costly victory. Lee was forced all the way back into Virginia.

Despite this hard-won victory, McClellan, who was a favorite with his men, had nonetheless fallen out of favor with the higher command. Generals Ambrose E. Burnside and Joseph "Fighting Joe" Hooker were given command of the army, and defeat plagued the Union until winter appeared.

People most likely thought 1863 would have seen the Union erring on the side of caution thanks to its defeats, even though it had succeeded in driving the Confederates back into the South. Instead, Lincoln proved that his mission of liberty would not be set back by anything. On New Year's Day, he issued the Emancipation Proclamation, and the slaves were officially freed at last. It was no longer legal for slaves to be kept anywhere in the United States of America. While the Confederates pushed back against the proclamation, it was nonetheless a moment that would shake the history of the US forever. Across the country, slaves broke free from their masters, thirsting for the liberty that was legally theirs, and they moved to the North in droves. Around 186,000 of them joined the Union as soldiers, determined to secure their freedom and that of their brothers and sisters forever.

Its ranks now swollen with newly freed people, the Union Army braced itself for another onslaught when the winter faded. Lee opened the 1863 campaigning season with a victory against Fighting Joe

Hooker that cost him nearly one-quarter of his army. On July 1ˢᵗ to 3ʳᵈ, 1863, Lee would fight his most devastating battle yet, clashing with General George G. Meade in the famous Battle of Gettysburg in Pennsylvania. American turned on American, and blood was shed in untold quantities, staining the peaceful earth there forever with the consequences of a nation's divide.

In the midst of the three-day-long battle, one brigade would lose many men yet still prove itself to be one of the greatest of the American Civil War. This was the Iron Brigade of the Union Army, known for their dashing appearance, disciplined fighting, and utter grit in the face of imminent death. The Iron Brigade was composed of Wisconsinites, Michiganders, and Indianans. Many of them were killed in the carnage, but when the battle finally ended, their deaths had not been in vain. The Confederates had lost nearly two-thirds of their army. Lee was forced to retreat, and this victory is much acknowledged as the turning point of the entire war.

Meade, however, would not be the only man in the Civil War to fight a powerful Union victory. In fact, the greatest and most well-known hero of the war was probably General Ulysses S. Grant. Although he was not yet the supreme commander by the summer of 1863, he nonetheless had control over a sizeable chunk of the army in Mississippi State. Like many Civil War generals, he always tried to have a regiment of Wisconsinites in his army; unlike many states, Wisconsin not only supplied plenty of volunteers in response to Lincoln's call to arms after the succession, but the state also replaced its soldiers when they were killed or lost. Wisconsinites established themselves as some of the most reliable men in the Union Army, none more so than the 8ᵗʰ Wisconsin Volunteer Infantry Regiment. Always accompanied by a bald eagle named Old Abe, who was the much-loved mascot of this regiment, the 8ᵗʰ Wisconsin was an instrumental part of Grant's army.

Accordingly, the regiment was a huge part of one of the Civil War's most important battles: the Siege of Vicksburg, which was fought from

May to July 1863. Weeks of siege and constant fighting couldn't defeat the 8th Wisconsin, and they took Vicksburg on July 4th, eighty-seven years to the day after the Declaration of Independence was signed. With the fall of Vicksburg came the beginning of the end for the Confederacy. The Union now had access to the Mississippi River and could control its banks, putting a stop to much of the river traffic and also cleaving the American South in half. The Confederates were now fighting a losing war.

Alongside another victory at the Battle of Chattanooga that November, the Siege of Vicksburg helped convince Lincoln that Grant was the right man for the daunting task of being supreme commander over the Union armies. In March 1864, Grant was given control of the entire Union force. He continued to fight battles in the East, and he was assisted in the West by General William Tecumseh Sherman. Although the spring of 1864 was plagued with defeat for Grant, Sherman showed that he had plenty of the warrior spirit his namesake was so famous for, as Southern cities fell one after the other to his armies. Atlanta, Georgia, was conquered in September 1864. Sherman pressed home his advantage and began the March to the Sea, moving his men all the way across the South toward the ocean, determined to claim every last blade of grass as Union territory.

Lee, for his part, had finally been made supreme commander of the Confederates. He had already proven his prowess throughout the war, and perhaps things would have been different if he had been the supreme commander from the time the first cannonball was launched into Fort Sumter. Now, though, it was much too late. His last victory was at Fort Stedman on March 25th, 1865, but Grant and Meade were hot on his heels and pushed him out of Fort Stedman and back to Richmond, Virginia.

In a matter of weeks, Lee was pushed all the way along the Appomattox River. He was running out of men, morale, resources, and—crucially—space. There was just nowhere left to retreat to, and after four years of warfare, Lee finally had to accept his defeat. He surrendered to Grant at the Appomattox Court House on April 9th.

Victory was close at hand. Across the Northern United States, celebrations broke out, as the joyous Union realized they had finally set America free. But their joy was tragically short-lived. On April 14th, while attending a play, Abraham Lincoln was shot in cold blood by John Wilkes Booth. He died the next day.

However, Lincoln's fervent beliefs in liberty did not die with him. The last Confederate general surrendered to Sherman in North Carolina on April 26th, and the American Civil War finally came to an end.

The war had been a bitter, bloody, and terribly costly one. The American South was a shadow of its former glory. Its luscious plantations, sculpted landscapes, and stately mansions had been decimated by the constant violent presence of massive armies moving across it. Six hundred twenty thousand American soldiers died in total, an incomprehensible number. This was more than the number of Americans who had died in the Revolution and the War of 1812 combined. Thirty-eight thousand were African Americans who had joined the Union to fight for their freedom.

However, the cost was not without reward for those who believed in liberty. The 13th, 14th, and 15th Amendments were passed shortly after the end of the war, which not only freed all slaves throughout the United States and put a permanent end to legal slavery but also granted African Americans the right to vote (although they had much fighting to do before they could vote in peace).

While no major battles were fought in Wisconsin itself—it was too far north to be in the line of fire—Wisconsinites nonetheless played a crucial role in the Union victory. Without the courageous 8th Wisconsin at the Siege of Vicksburg or the sacrificial courage of the 2nd, 6th, and 7th Wisconsin in the Iron Brigade at Gettysburg, these two great victories might never have been won. The Civil War would have looked very different.

Wisconsin's men perished in the thousands during the war; so many of them had been sent to the front that women had to step up and keep the state running during the war. Their efforts to care for their homes and families, as well as farming and keeping the rest of the state's industry at work, helped to keep the Union's resources running high. Logs, lead, and food all kept on coming from Wisconsin, thanks to the brave efforts of the women left behind. They also sent many donations of food, clothing, bedding, and other necessities to their "brave boys" on the front lines. Many new recruits also trained at Camp Randall, the modern-day stadium of the University of Wisconsin-Madison.

Despite the fact that none of the Civil War's blood was shed on its soil, Wisconsin was still deeply affected by the war. When it was all over, and its scarred and battered men could finally traipse back to the peaceful forests and green hills they'd left behind four years before, more than 12,000 Wisconsinites had died in the battles. As the entire United States began to find its feet in a new, post-Civil War world, almost torn apart from the inside out, Wisconsin showed its powerful resilience. With the war over, it blossomed during what we now call the Gilded Age. Industries boomed across the state, particularly in agriculture and brewing (leading to the birth of some of America's favorite beers, such as Miller, Pabst, and Leinenkugel). Wisconsin's economic growth was huge, allowing for plenty of employment opportunities and prosperity across the state.

Logging was a key part of the rising Gilded Age. But logging was also almost its downfall. Natural disasters were about to strike Wisconsin in its most raw and violent form: fire.

Chapter 6 – Wisconsin Burns

Illustration IV: Sterling Hall shortly after it was bombed in 1970

Father Peter Pernin's entire world seemed to be consumed by fire.

Everything was burning. Through streaming eyes assaulted by smoke, the priest could barely see as he stumbled along the bank of the Peshtigo River. The smoke was everywhere: a thick, black curtain that blinded his eyes and clogged his lungs, making every breath a fresh stab of torture as it sent agony through his chest. It was late at night, yet wherever Father Pernin looked, a sullen scarlet glow etched brutal details into the world. The reflection of flames on water. The desperation in the eyes of a lost horse, galloping along the road above the riverbank, heading right back toward the flames, its instinct calling it back to its stable even though fire lined its path. The body of a child, crushed and trampled by panicked feet fleeing before the blaze.

Father Pernin could barely comprehend what he was seeing. He'd poured his heart and soul into this frontier town, which many considered to be a godless den of villains. To be fair, only a few hours ago, he'd heard men laughing and carousing in the boarding house right near his home. But now, destruction was upon it, and Father Pernin had seen more death in the past half-hour than he could process.

There was a terrible crack from somewhere up the river. Father Pernin turned in time to see the bridge across the river, its timbers blazing as flames flickered across the ruined wood, begin to fall apart. The fire seemed to enjoy the groan of the bridge, sparks leaping up in exuberance as the bridge folded. As Father Pernin watched, the bridge collapsed into the water in a cloud of smoke, sparks, and ash. Debris swept downstream, the river already churning gray.

A cry of dismay rose from the parched throats of the people of Peshtigo. They were everywhere, clutching children and belongings as they hurried down the road or crowded next to the river, desperate to flee. The bridge had seemed like their only escape. But looking around him, at a sky filled with fire, and hearing the terrible roar of the flames, Father Pernin was starting to think that maybe there was no escape. Maybe this was the very end of the world.

Father Pernin took a deep breath. Even though many of Peshtigo's residents looked down on him for being Catholic, he believed fervently in God, and he had worked hard to bring what he believed to be hope and joy to these people. Right now, whether this was the end of the world or not, he had to do something for the people he loved.

Lungs burning, body aching, and skin blistering with heat, Father Pernin began to walk down the riverbank, pushing the dazed and panicked people of Peshtigo into the safety of the river. They were so confused by the destruction they witnessed that they couldn't think to take those few steps into the water. Father Pernin shoved them in one by one; he wanted to shout to them, to tell them to save themselves, but his throat was so raw from the smoke he'd inhaled that he couldn't utter a word. He didn't know if any of them could survive. He didn't know if the earth itself would survive. All he knew was that disaster was upon them.

A disaster on a scale that no one had ever seen before.

The Great Fire of Peshtigo

In 1871, Wisconsin was deep within its Gilded Age, and much of that era of economic growth was centered upon the logging industry. The growing population of the rest of the United States had an insatiable appetite for lumber. Houses, railroads, churches, schools, ships, books, newspapers—all of these had to be constructed from trees. And trees were something that Wisconsin had in wonderful abundance.

Peshtigo, located on the shore of Green Bay, only a few miles from the booming city of Green Bay, was a town devoted to the logging industry. It had been built on land owned by a wealthy logging tycoon named William Ogden not long before, and the town was growing so quickly that buildings seemed to pop up overnight. People flocked to Peshtigo to cut down its trees or work in the factory that processed them. In fact, Peshtigo's factory was the largest of its kind in the United States.

Like the rest of Wisconsin, Peshtigo had experienced an influx of immigrants, many of them from Scandinavian countries. Job opportunities were plentiful throughout the state. Land could be acquired cheaply, but for those who couldn't afford land, there was plenty of work to be had on the farms and forests. Lumberjacks lived in and around Peshtigo, many of them in tiny shanties among the trees that provided them with a living. Only a few were alone; many had young families with them. Their lives were hard, yet they'd left behind an overcrowded Old World in the throes of the Victorian Era. At least here they could breathe fresh air in a free country.

The logging industry had given these people a new lease on life; however, it would prove to be deadly to so many of them. Wherever loggers passed, they left behind tantalizing areas consisting of brush and stumps, its earth rich and good for farming if only those stumps could be cleared away. Farmers, hungry to join in Wisconsin's booming agricultural sector, looked for a quick solution to clear the land. Slash-and-burn became the norm. Acres of land were set alight in order to clear it for tilling and planting. Forest fires were a part of life for the people of Peshtigo; it wasn't uncommon for the sky to be shrouded by smoke for days at a time. Water barrels were brought up from the river and placed around the town, so the people managed to keep their homes safe.

But in 1871, a culmination of factors built a disaster so mind-boggling that human hands could have never hoped to prevent it. The summer of 1871 was a desperately dry one, leaving the woods parched. Every leaf, every fallen twig was perfect tinder, fuel for Peshtigo's impending doom. Despite this, farmers continued to burn stumps to clear their land. One fire after the other spiraled out of control. By October, the woods were so dry that spontaneous combustion became a possibility. It wasn't long before all those little fires were starting to meet up, to come together into one of nature's most unstoppable phenomena: a firestorm.

The firestorm first reached the little town of Sugar Bush on October 8th, 1871. Sugar Bush no longer exists; when the hungry flames reached the tiny village, they left nothing but ashes behind. People, animals, buildings—everything was completely destroyed in the fire.

From Sugar Bush, it swept on to Peshtigo, and by the time it reached the town, it had become something the likes of which humanity has never seen since. The firestorm had been whipped into a "firenado," a great twisting column of smoke, flame, and air so hot that it boiled sap inside trees, causing them to explode. The air heated to the point where birds in flight burst aflame, turning to ash before their bodies could hit the ground. Witnesses describe the sound as incomprehensibly loud; it was as if nature itself had gained a voice and spoken out against the atrocities that humanity had wrought upon it ever since the days of the Ice Age when Paleo-Indians hunted the mastodons.

By the time Father Pernin reached the banks of the Peshtigo, disaster was already upon his home. People fled the town in a panic, bringing whatever they could take with them. Those who reached the river were the lucky ones; the unlucky were trampled in the fray or outpaced by the flames, which burned them alive. Some never even made it out of their homes. Deep in their drunken sleep, the people Father Pernin had heard carousing next to his home all died—seventy-five tragic deaths, all from one building.

Even the river offered little protection against the flames. Father Pernin spent the night splashing water over his head, trying to stay alive. Many people died of smoke inhalation even though they were in the water; others were swept away and drowned in the current or succumbed to hypothermia after hours spent in the water.

By the time the fire had passed through Peshtigo and eventually burned itself out on the edge of Green Bay, the damage was almost incomprehensible. Peshtigo had been razed to the ground. Only heaps of soot and ash remained. The factory was gone, and Father

Pernin's church had been burned in such heat that the brass church bell was a melted pool. Sugar Bush was simply gone. Marinette, a nearby town, had also been affected.

It is impossible to say how many people died in the Great Fire of Peshtigo. Since entire towns were wiped out, records are scarce, and we simply don't know how many people had been living there in the first place. As many as 2,500 people may have perished, making the Great Peshtigo Fire the deadliest in known history. Damages totaled around $5,000,000, not including the destroyed crops and dead livestock.

Strangely enough, despite its extreme deadliness and the vivid accounts of its eyewitnesses, the Great Fire of Peshtigo has become a somewhat obscure event in history. This was because of a tragic coincidence. The very night that Peshtigo was burning, so was Chicago. The next day, the newspapers were filled with stories of the Great Chicago Fire, and Peshtigo was practically ignored, even though the fire in Chicago only killed around 300 people.

Peshtigo was eventually rebuilt. It is now a small but vibrant community, with a museum dedicated to the fire that destroyed it. As for Father Pernin, after having supported his congregation for several months directly after the fire, he continued to serve as a priest for the rest of his life elsewhere in the Great Lakes area.

The Sterling Hall Bombing

Ninety-nine years later, Wisconsin was burning once more.

Two young brothers—aged nineteen and twenty-two—sat in a yellow Corvair and watched as a great fireball rose into the night. It bloomed like a great rose of glowing flame, laced by tracks of gray smoke, casting an eerie glow upon the city of Madison, whose people slumbered that summer night.

In the Corvair, Dwight Armstrong's heart was thundering as he sat in the passenger seat beside his brother Karleton, known as Karl to his friends. Dwight could hardly believe that he'd really done it. He'd bombed Sterling Hall, a part of the University of Wisconsin-Madison. The feeling was an intoxicating rush of pride and adrenaline, a powerful emotion that he'd done something right. Dwight had stood up for something that he fiercely believed in.

It had seemed simple enough at the start. With Karl's help, it hadn't been hard to buy some fuel oil from one agricultural cooperative and a whole lot of fertilizer from another. The materials were easy to make into a bomb; they combined them with just a little dynamite and a fuse, and then they packed it into a stolen Ford van. Dwight had driven the Ford and parked it strategically beside Sterling Hall, home to the mathematics department of the University of Wisconsin-Madison, which had been helping to build weapons that were being used in Vietnam.

Like many young people of the 1970s, Dwight was deeply opposed to the Vietnam War. Although many Wisconsinites like him had served in the two world wars that had consumed the first half of the 20th century, Dwight was a generation late for that, being born after the Second World War had ended. His world seemed populated with older people for whom war was part of normality. But for Dwight, it all just felt wrong.

Unfortunately for peace advocates like him, the world was used to war. The two world wars had given way to the simmering tension of the Cold War and the terrible violence of its proxy wars, one of the most prominent among being the war in Vietnam. While the US was pouring soldiers into Vietnam in the name of defeating communism, young people at home were starting to wonder if all the violence was necessary. Anti-war protests had burst out across the country, and some of them had grown violent.

Dwight had been a peaceful protester up until just a few months ago. While other protest groups had been setting off bombs to destroy property, not people, Dwight had been content to express his opinions in marches and rallies. That was until a protest in Ohio had gone horribly south on May 4th. Tensions had erupted, and the

National Guard opened fire on the young protesters, killing four students right in front of Dwight's eyes. The sight had appalled him and flipped a switch inside. Dwight the peaceful protester had become Dwight the bomber.

Still, although his veins surged with adrenaline as Karl revved up the Corvair to leave and meet their two co-conspirators—nineteen-year-old David S. Fine and twenty-two-year-old Leo F. Burt—to celebrate their success with a Coke, Dwight felt a scrap of reassurance. Although what he'd done was illegal, at least no one was hurt. Dwight had checked in the windows of the building himself, and he and Karl had chosen their time—3:42 in the morning—because they were sure that there would be no one inside the building.

Sadly, they'd been horribly wrong. A radio report just a few minutes into their celebration shattered Dwight's world. Someone had died in the explosion: a young grad student, a thirty-three-year-old married man who had three little kids, named Robert Fassnacht. To make matters even worse, Fassnacht had been anti-war too. And now he was dead. And Dwight was a murderer.

Dwight and Karl fled to New York, their names now on the FBI's most wanted list. The two young men had only meant to express their discontent over the war in Vietnam, but instead, they'd killed one man and injured three others.

Ultimately, Karl would be captured in Toronto in 1972, leading to a twenty-three-year prison sentence, although he only spent seven years behind bars. Eventually, he would settle into a peaceful life, running a variety of small businesses in Madison; one of these was a deli called Radical Rye, which he co-owned with Dwight. Dwight himself had also served some time in prison. He passed away in 2010 from lung cancer.

David Fine also served three years in prison before going on to study law, although he was never admitted to the bar. He passed the exam, but his involvement in the bombing led to the denial of his admission.

The final bomber, Leo Burt, went into hiding and was never found.

Progression in Wisconsin during the 20ᵗʰ Century

Wisconsin had changed hugely since the Peshtigo Fire. Industries like logging and agriculture had declined in importance, giving rise to a thriving economy based on services instead. Wisconsin was now—and, in many ways, still is—a center of education and medicine.

Yet the progressive ideas and proud idealism that had borne it through the American Civil War were still very much evident. In fact, Wisconsin's politics were some of the most progressive in the entire US, and it invented concepts that have become an integral part of the modern world, concepts like income tax and workplace compensation for injuries or unemployment. The "Wisconsin Idea," first expressed in 1905 by the president of the University of Wisconsin-Madison, had given rise to the broadly accepted thought that universities should work to benefit all residents of their local areas and beyond, not just its students. As a result, the University of Wisconsin-Extension was established, and education at many levels was offered to all kinds of people within the state.

It's unsurprising then, given its reputation as a state filled with progressive ideas, that Wisconsin was the center of many anti-war protests. It had long sought to benefit its young people, welcome their ideas, and provide them with education. These protests and the peace movement in many ways defined the 1970s and 1980s.

Sadly, however, Dwight and Karl Armstrong's bombing of Sterling Hall had exactly the opposite effect they had intended. These two young men had crossed a terrible line: they'd accidentally killed someone in the very act of speaking out against killings. Other peace protesters were horrified by what had happened and were abruptly made aware that the destruction of property could easily become the accidental destruction of life. After 1970, protests began to decline all over the United States.

The Vietnam War, however, would rage on for years, finally ending in 1975.

Conclusion

Today, Wisconsin's economy has given a nod to its Gilded Age, returning to its old industries of agriculture and logging, which make up the bulk of its economy. It is particularly well known for its many large dairy farms and production of cheese, although information technology and tourism are also important parts of the economy. In terms of politics, Wisconsin has a Democrat governor at the time of writing. Thus, Wisconsin, the birthplace of the Republican Party, still upholds the same virtues the original Republican Party once upheld, as the Democrats and Republicans slowly switched ideologies over the centuries. However, the two parties are in hot competition during elections, with the state regularly changing hands.

It is never for sure which political party will be the next to preside over Wisconsin. One thing that is for sure, though, is that Wisconsinites will always be Wisconsinites. Despite a rocky start, with the early American settlers waging war on Native Americans and even on each other during the debacle of the Milwaukee bridges, Wisconsin's people have since proven themselves as free thinkers. These are the people who liberated Joshua Glover, the people who fueled the American Civil War, the people who rebuilt so many of their towns from the ashes of the Great Fire of Peshtigo.

These are the Wisconsinites. And their story is one of hope for a better future.

Here's another book by Captivating History that you might like

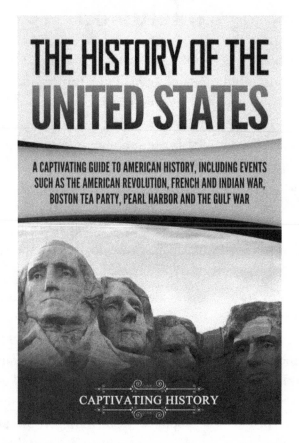

Free Bonus from Captivating History
(Available for a Limited time)

Hi History Lovers!

Now you have a chance to join our exclusive history list so you can get your first history ebook for free as well as discounts and a potential to get more history books for free! Simply visit the link below to join.

Captivatinghistory.com/ebook

Also, make sure to follow us on Facebook, Twitter and Youtube by searching for Captivating History.

Sources

Little, B. 2018, *Why Did the Clovis People Mysteriously Vanish?*, A&E Television Networks, viewed 26 August 2020 <https://www.history.com/news/clovis-migration-discovery>

Weiser-Alexander, K. 2020, *Clovis Culture of Native Americans*, Legends of America, viewed 26 August 2020, <https://www.legendsofamerica.com/clovis-culture/>

Wisconsin Historical Society 2008, *Paleo-Indian Fluted Spear Point*, Wisconsin Historical Society Press, viewed 26 August 2020, <https://www.wisconsinhistory.org/Records/Article/CS2656>

Tyrrell, K. A. 2016, *The Mysterious Mastodon*, On Wisconsin, viewed 26 August 2020, <https://onwisconsin.uwalumni.com/features/the-mysterious-mastodon/>

Jovaag, S. 2015, *Geologists Rewrite the Story of Wisconsin's Boaz Mastodon*, Wisconsin Life, viewed 26 August 2020, <https://www.wisconsinlife.org/story/geologists-rewrite-the-story-of-wisconsins-boaz-mastodon/>

Tyrrell, K. A. 2015, *Rewriting the history of the Boaz Mastodon*, University of Wisconsin-Madison, viewed 26 August 2020, <https://news.wisc.edu/rewriting-the-history-of-the-boaz-mastodon/>

Cullen, K. M. 2006, *Old Copper Culture*, Milwaukee Public Museum, viewed 26 August 2020, <https://www.mpm.edu/research-collections/anthropology/online-collections-research/old-copper-culture>

Wisconsin Historical Society, *Exploring the History of Aztalan*, Wisconsin Historical Society, viewed 26 August 2020, <https://www.wisconsinhistory.org/Records/Article/CS4051>

Hirst, K. K. 2020, *The Oneota Culture – Last Prehistoric Culture of the American Midwest*, ThoughtCo, viewed 26 August 2020, <https://www.thoughtco.com/oneota-culture-of-the-american-midwest-167045>

Hirst, K. K. 2017, *Cahokia (USA) – Massive Mississippian Center in the American Bottom*, ThoughtCo, viewed 26 August 2020, <https://www.thoughtco.com/prehistoric-cahokia-usa-170438>

Native History Association, *The Mississippian Period*, NativeHistoryAssociation.org, viewed 26 August 2020, <http://www.nativehistoryassociation.org/mississippian.php>

Wisconsin Historical Society, *Effigy Mounds Culture*, Wisconsin Historical Society, viewed 26 August 2020, <https://www.wisconsinhistory.org/Records/Article/CS383>

Canadian Museum of History, *Jean Nicollet 1634*, Virtual Museum of New France, viewed 27 August 2020, <https://www.historymuseum.ca/virtual-museum-of-new-france/the-explorers/jean-nicollet-1634/>

History.com Editors 2020, *Exploration of North America*, A&E Television Networks, viewed 27 August 2020, <https://www.history.com/topics/exploration/exploration-of-north-america>

The Editors of the Encyclopedia Britannica 2020, *Jean Nicolet*, Encyclopedia Britannica, viewed 27 August 2020, <https://www.britannica.com/biography/Jean-Nicolet>

Wien, T. 2020, *Nicolet, Explorations of,* Encyclopedia.com, viewed 27 August 2020, <https://www.encyclopedia.com/people/history/us-history-biographies/jean-nicolet>

Le Canada: A People's History, *Radisson and des Groseilliers*, CBC, viewed 27 August 2020, <https://www.cbc.ca/history/EPCONTENTSE1EP6CH1PA3LE.html>

Canadian Museum of History, *Medard Chouart des Groseilliers 1654-1660,* Virtual Museum of New France, viewed 27 August 2020, <https://www.historymuseum.ca/virtual-museum-of-new-france/the-explorers/medard-chouart-des-groseilliers-1654-1660/>

Anonymous 2020, *Allouez, Claude Jean*, New Catholic Encyclopedia, viewed 27 August 2020, <https://www.encyclopedia.com/religion/encyclopedias-almanacs-transcripts-and-maps/allouez-claude-jean>

Wisconsin Historical Society, *Allouez, Claude Jean (1622-1689),* Wisconsin Historical Society, viewed 27 August 2020, <https://www.wisconsinhistory.org/Records/Article/CS2822>

Link, M. 1937, *The Missionary Labors and Travels of Father Claude Jean Allouez, S. J.*, Loyola University Chicago eCommons, viewed 27 August 2020, <https://core.ac.uk/download/pdf/48598365.pdf>

Wisconsin Historical Society, *Nicolas Perrot: French Fur Trade in Wisconsin*, Wisconsin Historical Society, viewed 27 August 2020, <https://www.wisconsinhistory.org/Records/Article/CS541>

Canadian Museum of History, *Nicolas Perrot 1665-1689,* Virtual Museum of New France, viewed 27 August 2020, <https://www.historymuseum.ca/virtual-museum-of-new-france/the-explorers/nicolas-perrot-1665-1689/>

Anonymous, *Beaver Wars*, Ohio History Central, viewed 27 August 2020, <http://ohiohistorycentral.org/w/Beaver_Wars>

Wisconsin Historical Society, *Fox Wars, 1712-1730*, Wisconsin Historical Society, viewed 31 August 2020, https://www.wisconsinhistory.org/Records/Article/CS1728

Grignon, A. 1857, *Seventy-two years of recollections of Wisconsin*, State Historical Society of Wisconsin, via Wisconsin Historical Society, viewed 31 August 2020, <https://content.wisconsinhistory.org/digital/collection/whc/id/1441>

Daniels, R. C. 2019, *The 1712-1736 Fox Wars: The Fox Indians and the French battle over the fur trade*, Military History Online, viewed 31 August 2020, <militaryhistoryonline.com/Century18th/FoxWars>

Griffith, W. R. IV, *The French and Indian War (1754-1763): Causes and Outbreak*, American Battlefield Trust, viewed 31 August 2020, <https://www.battlefields.org/learn/articles/french-and-indian-war-1754-1763-causes-and-outbreak>

History.com Editors 2020, *French and Indian War*, A&E Television Networks, viewed 31 August 2020, <https://www.history.com/topics/native-american-history/french-and-indian-war>

Encyclopedia of the American Revolution: Library of Military History 2020, *Langlade, Charles Michel de*, Encyclopedia.com, viewed 31 August 2020, <https://www.encyclopedia.com/people/history/us-history-biographies/charles-michel-de-langlade>

Gould, H. 2014, *Jonathan Carver: explorer, mapmaker, author and subject of controversy*, MinnPost, viewed 31 August 2020, <https://www.minnpost.com/mnopedia/2014/01/jonathan-carver-explorer-mapmaker-author-and-subject-controversy/>

History.com Editors 2019, *Revolutionary War*, A&E Television Networks, viewed 3 September 2020, <https://www.history.com/topics/american-revolution/american-revolution-history>

History.com Editors 2020, *British Parliament adopts the Coercive Acts in response to the Boston Tea Party*, A&E Television Networks, viewed 3 September 2020, <https://www.history.com/this-day-in-history/british-parliament-adopts-the-coercive-acts>

Wisconsin Historical Society, *Battle of Prairie du Chien, 1814,* Wisconsin Historical Society, viewed 3 September 2020, <https://www.wisconsinhistory.org/Records/Article/CS1696>

American Battlefield Trust website, viewed 3 September 2020, <https://www.battlefields.org/>

Anderson, Thomas Gummersall. "The British Capture Prairie du Chien during the War of 1812." From the Draper Manuscripts at the Wisconsin Historical Society, (Draper 1Q241-250); online facsimile at http://www.wisconsinhistory.org/turningpoints/search.asp?id=26

Wolly, B. and Horwitz, T. 2012, *The 10 Things You Didn't Know About the War of 1812,* Smithsonian Magazine, viewed 3 September 2020, <https://www.smithsonianmag.com/history/the-10-things-you-didnt-know-about-the-war-of-1812-102320130/>

History.com Editors 2020, *War of 1812,* A&E Television Networks, viewed 3 September 2020, <https://www.history.com/topics/war-of-1812/war-of-1812>

Andrews, E. 2018, *How the Battle of Tippecanoe Helped Win the White House,* A&E Television Networks, viewed 3 September 2020, <https://www.history.com/news/how-the-battle-of-tippecanoe-helped-win-the-white-house>

Smith, R. B. 1998, *Black Hawk War,* HistoryNet, viewed 3 September 2020, <https://www.historynet.com/black-hawk-war>

Wisconsin Historical Society, *Winnebago War (1827),* Wisconsin Historical Society, viewed 3 September 2020, <https://www.wisconsinhistory.org/Records/Article/CS1833>

History.com Editors 2020, *Black Hawk War begins,* A&E Television Networks, viewed 3 September 2020, <https://www.history.com/this-day-in-history/black-hawk-war-begins>

Vogt, M., *The Black Hawk War*, Iowa Pathways, viewed 3 September 2020, <http://www.iowapbs.org/iowapathways/mypath/black-hawk-war>

TerBeek, E. 2015, *Old Milwaukee: The Bridge War of 1845, And How the Streets Got Their Names*, Milwaukee Record, viewed 3 September 2020, <https://milwaukeerecord.com/city-life/old-milwaukee-the-bridge-war-of-1845-and-how-the-streets-got-their-names/>

Renda, L., *Bridge War*, Encyclopedia of Milwaukee, viewed 3 September 2020, <https://emke.uwm.edu/entry/bridge-war/>

Milwaukee Historical Society website: <https://milwaukeehistory.net/education/milwaukee-timeline/>

History.com Editors 2020, *Boston Massacre*, A&E Television Networks, viewed 3 September 2020, <https://www.history.com/topics/american-revolution/boston-massacre>

History.com Editors 2019, *Wisconsin enters the Union*, A&E Television Networks, viewed 10 September 2020, <https://www.history.com/this-day-in-history/wisconsin-enters-the-union>

Sobel, Robert, and John Raimo, eds. Biographical Directory of the Governors of the United States, 1789-1978, Vol. 4. Westport, CT: Meckler Books, 1978. 4 vols.

The National Cyclopaedia of American Biography, Vol. 12. New York: James T. White & Company.

Wisconsin Historical Society. Wisconsin Local History & Biography Articles; Lancaster Teller; Cassville; Wisconsin; 1889

Cross, S. 1929, *Birthplace of the Republican Party*, Oshkosh Public Museum, viewed 10 September 2020, <https://oshkosh.pastperfectonline.com/photo/794D42F0-FE01-483D-B859-650599355293>

History.com Editors 2020, *Republican Party*, A&E Television Networks, viewed 10 September 2020, <https://www.history.com/topics/us-politics/republican-party>

History.com Editors 2019, *Kansas-Nebraska Act*, A&E Television Networks, viewed 10 September 2020, <https://www.history.com/topics/19th-century/kansas-nebraska-act>

Rogan, A. 2020, *A look back: The story of Joshua Glover and how Racine freed him from slavery in 1854*, The Journal Times, viewed 10 September 2020, <https://journaltimes.com/news/local/a-look-back-the-story-of-joshua-glover-and-how-racine-freed-him-from-slavery/article_06007066-31af-5a66-a693-26f16554088d.html>

Wisconsin Historical Society, *Joshua Glover*, Wisconsin Historical Society, viewed 10 September 2020, <https://www.wisconsinhistory.org/Records/Article/CS4368>

Wisconsin Historical Society, *Booth, Sherman Miller (1812-1904)*, Wisconsin Historical Society, viewed 10 September 2020, <https://www.wisconsinhistory.org/Records/Article/CS5621>

Hickman, K. 2020, *American Civil War 101*, ThoughtCo, viewed 10 September 2020, <https://www.thoughtco.com/american-civil-war-a-short-history-2360921>

History.com Editors 2020, *Civil War*, A&E Television Networks, viewed 10 September 2020, <https://www.history.com/topics/american-civil-war/american-civil-war-history>

Vogeler, I. G. 2020, *Wisconsin*, Encyclopedia Britannica, viewed 14 September 2020, <https://www.britannica.com/place/Wisconsin>

Pernin, P. 1917, *The Great Peshtigo Fire: An Eyewitness Account*, Wisconsin Historical Society

Bromley, B. 2014, *Aftershocks: Local ties to Sterling Hall bombing remembered*, Baraboo News Republic, viewed 14 September 2020, <https://www.wiscnews.com/baraboonewsrepublic/news/local/aftersho

cks-local-ties-to-sterling-hall-bombing-remembered/article_74da5325-7a35-5669-aeec-33e6ec66a460.html>

Fox, M. 2010, *Dwight Armstrong, Who Bombed a College Building in 1970, Dies at 58*, The New York Times, viewed 14 September 2020, <https://www.nytimes.com/2010/06/27/us/27armstrong.html>

Anonymous 2017, *Why Few Remember the Peshtigo Fire, The Deadliest in American History*, All That's Interesting, viewed 14 September 2020, <https://allthatsinteresting.com/peshtigo-fire>

History.com Editors 2019, *Massive fire burns in Wisconsin*, A&E Television Networks, viewed 14 September 2020, <https://www.history.com/this-day-in-history/massive-fire-burns-in-wisconsin>

Estep, K., *The Peshtigo Fire*, Green Bay Press-Gazette, viewed 14 September 2020, <https://www.weather.gov/grb/peshtigofire>

Illustration I:
https://commons.wikimedia.org/wiki/File:Jean_Nicolet_Landing_in_Wisconsin,_July_1634,_Milwaukee_Public_Museum_(NBY_22648).jpg

Illustration II:
https://upload.wikimedia.org/wikipedia/commons/a/af/Stillman%27s_Run_Battle_Site_Black_Hawk_War_memorial.jpg

Illustration III: By Unknown author -
https://www.wisconsinhistory.org/Records/Image/IM41960, Public Domain,
https://commons.wikimedia.org/w/index.php?curid=58373781

Illustration IV:
https://upload.wikimedia.org/wikipedia/commons/a/a4/Sterling_Hall_bombing_after_explosion_1.jpg